Sudha Koul was born into a Hindu family in Kashmir, a predomi-
nantly Muslim valley, in the year of India's partition. She was educated
first in an Irish nuns' school, then a women's college and state
university. She became the first Kashmiri woman selected to the
Indian Administrative Service, with hundreds of villages under her
jurisdiction. Since the 1980s the idyllic Kashmir of her childhood has
been ripped apart by religious bigotry and political mismanagement.
Sudha Koul now lives in America.

SUDHA KOUL

The Tiger Ladies

A MEMOIR OF KASHMIR

review

First published in 2002
by REVIEW

An imprint of Headline Book Publishing

First published in the United States of America in 2002
by Beacon Press, Boston

10 9 8 7 6 5 4 3 2 1

Cataloguing in Publication Data is available from the British Library

ISBN 0 7553 1116 7

Text design by Melodie Wertelet/mwdesign

Composition by Wilsted & Taylor Publishing Services

Kashmiri shawl reproduced on front cover supplied by
Paisley Museum Service

Printed and bound in Great Britain by
Clays Ltd, St Ives plc

HEADLINE BOOK PUBLISHING
A division of Hodder Headline
338 Euston Road
LONDON NW1 3BH

www.reviewbooks.co.uk
www.hodderheadline.com

For Shyamji, Dhanna and Babuji, Tathaji,
and other ancestors who exhort me to
write what might very well turn out to be
an epitaph to a way of life.

And for Clarissa Pinkola Estes,
who does not know me.

Acknowledgements

Thank you Agha Shahid Ali for saying 'This book must be published'.
I will miss you forever. Thank you Rosalie Siegel, Helene Atwan,
Louise Greenberg and Lindsay Symons for helping me make sure
someone will hear the tree fall. Thank you my beloved family, Kishen
(my honest sounding-board), Keya (my remarkable in-home editor),
and Yashomati (my fiercely loyal supporter).

Who has not heard of the Vale of Cashmere?

Thomas Moore, *Lalla Rookh* (1817)

Grandmothers

Om! Shri Ganeshaye Namah!

With that invocation made right at the beginning we make sure that everything shall turn out well.

Time unravels like a dog's tail, then it curls right back into a circle, and you start all over again. As we live out our lives, we gaze at the heavens and stumble on the nearest rock, and then we pull ourselves up, dust off the sand, and look around us. We think we have taken stock, we know our parameters, our landscape, and then our eyes go skyward again. If we were to look back we would see a disappearing line of predecessors whose lifetimes we have unknowingly mimicked. We look up eagerly at our gods instead and we live in hope.

My grandmother, Dhanna, has a mouth that smells like babies, all milky, toothless, and harmless, except when she smokes her hookah. She of the crisply washed cotton dress dried on the grass in the sun; her clothes smell of the herbs of spring and summer, and of the earth; she makes buttermilk drinks all day. Dhanna sits there at her kitchen window, one knee on the seasoned sill, the other knee balancing a round metal pot in which she whips up buttermilk flavored with salt and dried mint powder. I watch her make white and green foam as she churns the wooden whisk between her cracked dry palms.

The mint is from her grandfather's well. The leaves are

plucked, then washed and dried on the wood-shingled rooftop. When the mint is so dry that it crumbles to the touch it is powdered by a small round stone mortar in an oval pestle, both of which have blackened with use and time.

"The well water is so pure that it makes the leaves fragrant," says my mother's mother, Dhanna. "You must have mint buttermilk drinks in summer. It cools everything," she says, although she drinks glasses of her concoction even in winter because she thinks women must always have buttermilk or yogurt. But in summer she churns the sweet elixir all day, and offers it to everyone who walks in her wooden door, bending a little as they enter her well-worn portal.

Sometimes my grandmother fries brook trout in a small pan on a hissing kerosene stove. The stove is set on a reed mat in her cold, dark kitchen, and all the windows are shut. When she cooks fish she opens the wooden windows only if she must. Like so many others in our valley of Kashmir, she does not want a stranger's glance falling on her fish.

She tells me, "Of all things fish are the most susceptible to the evil eye."

No one must know, so the wooden windowpanes of her kitchen keep the smell inside. The kitchen looks like a dungeon. Instead of turning on the electric light I open up all the windows and let the sunlight pour in, revealing corners and bits of dust under the furniture. She allows me to do anything I want to and all is forgiven. I am the firstborn of her first surviving child. Let me explain.

Dhanna, of the fierce temper, and my grandfather Babuji of the ready laugh and reflective nature, both dream of the children they will have. She is young, unlettered, and outspoken. Her office-going husband is quiet, a complete householder, but he also practices his own austerities and rituals. She is dainty and light and from the city, and he is heavy and dark and from the village, and they have found each other in their marriage. Everything exists around their union. He is entranced by everything she does. They say, behind his back, that he indulges her. And does she have a temper, they say.

Together my grandparents pray for children. She runs her palm over her full belly many times but then somehow the children are lost, either inside her or after she lets them go. Then the husband and wife wait, year after year, and pray for the children they will keep.

One night Dhanna has a dream and she is told what she has to do to keep her children. So she goes to the village of her ancestors. She finds a well at least nine-men deep and it is near her mother's house. Once a month she goes to the well at midnight, unties the two tightly woven braids of hair that start just above the nape of her neck. With her fingers she pries open the strands until her hair, crimped by weeklong braiding, falls loosely about her shoulders. Then she takes a bath.

She draws the water herself, lowering the well post with the bucket dangling at the end into the cold silent well. Then, slowly she pulls out the water, and in the dark she can hear the reassuring licks of the water in the bucket as it comes to rest on the grass beside her. This she does for one year, bathing through the seasons, gritting her teeth as the Himalayan winter approaches, glad that her ritual is a monthly and not a daily one. If she had to do it every day she would.

She says, "When you have to do something, you do it." No one may see her, or she will have to start all over again.

After twelve baths at a forgotten well hidden by wild mint bushes, my mother's mother comes home to her husband. Then she conceives again. By autumn her belly has grown full and taut. She likes to sit under the fruit trees, and her lips are purple from the large black cherries she eats all day. They all say she will give birth to someone special; all she wants to eat is fruit. When it comes to children everyone looks for signs and portents.

Dhanna had fourteen children. She lost eleven of them before she found the way to keep them. That is when she had my mother, then my aunt followed a couple of years later, and a few years later she had my uncle. He was dressed as a girl and nursed under cover to fool the evil eye. As a child my uncle always had some black soot from the kitchen stoves rubbed on his forehead, like so many other children, girls and boys, to make him undesirable to fate. There was some discussion about naming him after a demon to achieve the same purpose, but in the end my grandparents decided to be up front about it and opted for calling him "longevity" instead.

My uncle eventually grew out of his mother's arms, and out of the girls' clothes, and became a deceptively fierce-looking man with a large mustache. My grandmother could not fool his destiny anymore. In spite of all her efforts he is, like all of us, tempting to his fate and she claims him. Grandmother resigns herself to her daughter-in-law, but never really forgives her for taking her son into a world that excludes her and where she cannot protect him.

Now I see her sucking at her hookah, puffing up the smoke through the water in the hookah-belly, her still-young eyes in an old face. She laughs at me, she prefers to treat me as if I am still a small child, she is unwilling to let go of the child. She throws the apron of her ankle-length *pheran* on my feet to make sure I am warm.

Her skin is ivory, dry and crinkled like parchment, reddish near the cheeks, as if someone has just dabbed colored powder under her lively eyes. She wears several large and heavy gold hoops in each of her ears, all through the same hole. The holes are stretched by the time I become a girl, and the only reason that her earlobes are not torn is that the hoops are also held up by a ribbon that goes over her head and takes some of the weight off her ears. Even so, the hole in her earlobe is stretched and large. I can catch glimpses of the nape of her neck through the hole in her earlobe as she makes quick movements and gesticulates. Her animation is also a cause for consternation among the other women because it is entrancing and you have to look at her. The men don't seem to mind. When her husband died they said she was a beautiful woman.

I stare at her and her colors and take in her textures and her smells. I know that I will not have them forever. She stares at me with contentment in her eyes. I am a hybrid, daughter of her daughter, two men are in the picture by the time I arrive, but her smile informs me that ultimately I am from her loins.

When I was born Dhanna brought all kinds of things for my mother to eat. For me she brought things to wear. My swaddling clothes are from her, an old pashmina shawl of natural color, almost threadbare but layered like phyllo, impossibly light, so warm and soft, and delicious to smell.

In our valley of Kashmir, which sits like an infant in the lap of the Himalayas, one of the first things you do when a newborn arrives is to make sure the baby is warm. You take the oldest shawl in the family, one that has worn fine with use, and fold it many times over until you have a small cloudlike blanket for the infant. The snow line encircles us and we are always making sure that we are warmed by wool and by firewood.

The men usually arrange for the procurement and purchase of firewood in the autumn when winter begins to nip at our heels. It is a short and brisk transaction. The wood is bought, chopped, and arranged in crisscross fashion in backyards, ready to provide the beneficence of heat for our rooms and cooking stoves when winter arrives. Wood from the *hatab* tree is at a premium because its density provides the most intense heat; walnut wood is highly prized as well, and nothing catches fire like the pine, but there comes a time in the winter when any wood is better than none at all. Not everyone can afford a wood-burning stove at home, but all carry their own *kangri,* a small handy portable firepot around which a basket with handles is woven in red and green wicker. If we are to survive the winter, we must carry the indispensable kangri everywhere. It warms our beds and dries small articles of clothing in winter; we warm milk in it in the metal *khos* we drink tea from; we burn incense in it at weddings, roast chestnuts or small pieces of meat in it; we light our hookah tobacco with its coals. In winter when we sit on a chair, very often our feet are resting on a kangri. When we sit on the carpet, our legs folded against our chest with our feet away from the body, the kangri is kept under our knees in the space between our feet and thighs, like a central heating system.

Wool, on the other hand, is a lifetime's preoccupation. Women and men collect pashmina and wool fabrics, they have woolen clothes stitched, they have woolens knitted, or they knit themselves. Kashmiri women used to weave their own pashmina, no one else knew the arcane technique that produced the inimitable weave. Now they have it done because no one seems to have the patience anymore. We too have a family spindle put away in the attic, covered with cobwebs. It may not hold any magic for the women in my family, but I have read a story about a dormant female and a kissing prince at my Irish convent school and stay away from it.

Dhanna is a collector of pashmina; she has great yards, medium-size shawls, and small pieces of the reassuring fabric. She sprinkles her collection with dried bitter flowers and medicinal herbs and wraps them in fine muslin. Then she wraps the muslin-covered bundle in hand-embroidered cotton or silk tablecloths and ties up the corners so that no air or silverfish can find their way into her hoard. As she gathers up the packages to put them into a large steel trunk, and locks up with a padlock, she repeats a litany I have heard to the point of not listening.

"Pashmina has always meant security for the women of Kashmir. In the old days women got saris of pashmina in their trousseaux, but they only wore everyday wool at home. If they fell upon bad days they cut a shawl out of a length of pashmina and sold it to the shawl peddler for cash. Never forget, these shawls are equal to gold." She says this with a sigh, softly, matter-of-factly, just as my mother will eventually.

My grandmother smoothes out the wrinkles in the fabric with a gentle reverence that is shared by all Kashmiris. We don't brag about it much, but we know that we have enslaved Europe and conquered Scotland with this silky wool made from the winter fleece of the goats found only in the upper reaches of our mountains. We have spun wisps of the elusive down, slowly, lovingly, and we would never have accepted the machine-made incarnation they named after our valley. In Kashmir the real thing is what we are after. If the women wear gold it is so pure that it turns soft like butter when they stand in front of the kitchen fires.

My grandmother's shawl peddler, like all our tradespeople, is a Muslim. We Hindus are all Brahmins and are commonly called pandits, denoting our tradition of being the learned caste. There are no other Hindu castes in the valley. Many explanations have been put forward for this unprecedented situation, so unlike the rest of India, where there are always several castes in each Hindu community. The most common explanation is that most of the Brahmins were administrators and did not have to convert to Islam or did not want to convert. Some pandits did convert and their descendants carry their Brahmin names today, even though they are Muslim.

Hindus form a minuscule minority in the valley, but I remember that it did not worry us a bit, we did not think that Muslims and Hindus were natural enemies. In Kashmir, we were more preoccupied with the fact that we were all Kashmiri and we lived in the most beautiful place on earth.

Like other visitors to the house, the shawl peddler takes off his shoes before he enters the kitchen hall and sits on the floor with the ladies of the house. It is always too cold to keep the floors bare, so we pad the floor with a cushioning reed *waguv*, over which embroidered, pressed-wool *namdeh* or layered *gab-*

beh are piled on for warmth, and, if you can afford them, carpets top off all the padding.

The shawl dealer is given a cup and saucer set aside especially for Muslims; one never knows what kinds of meats they eat at home. Hindus do not usually eat food touched by Muslims, so the question of sharing dishes does not arise. In any case my grandmother does not touch porcelain or china, even ours; she drinks her tea out of her goblet-shaped brass khos. In her scheme of things glass and metal are not forbidden and terra-cotta is fine.

"Not to be touched," she says, pointing to the bone china dishes in the china closet out in the dining room, dishes required for her husband's official visitors.

She is reluctant to say why because she cannot bring herself to say the sacrilegious words "crushed cows' bones." It is a rumor brought to us centuries ago from China and the mountains have trapped it, like so many other things, in the valley.

The shawl man is content not to drink tea from a Hindu cup; he does not know what has crossed their lips. Hindus habitually garnish their food with asafetida, which he, like many others, believes comes from pigs' feet. He can hardly bring himself to use those words. Nothing is said, no misgivings explained, these mutual misunderstandings are completely acceptable and completely in place.

All this religious stuff is irrelevant in light of the real business at hand. The peddler is privy to the innermost secrets of the household, because girls, pashmina, gold, silver, shawls, puberty, and marriage are all wrapped up in the same tender package, opened up only to the innermost members of a family circle. He carries his own bundles of exquisites, wrapped many times over, on his bicycle rack, as he pedals through the narrow lanes of the old city and through the wide streets of the new city where we now live. When he sits down, with some ceremony, to display what he has brought them, all the women of the house surround him.

The shawl wallah takes embroidery orders based on his prized silk samplers that are over a hundred years old. His village has grown the fat white cocoons of the silkworm on mulberry leaves since the days of the Chinese traders. No one remembers the silk traders anymore, but we continue to grow silk, weave it, walk on it, and wear it, and it lasts forever. His family has sent its silk carpets around the world for generations, but he loves the shawl trade. It suits him, he is part of every step of the interpretation and execution of the designs he owns, and his collection of samplers is his claim to fame. Besides, carpets take months to weave and the young weavers follow a song pattern that is sung for them out of a tattered book, day in and day out, by an old master sitting on the side. The shawl peddler is too fond of company, frequent compliments; he is restless and energetic and too much his own person to follow patterns composed in their entirety centuries ago.

With a quick flick of his wrist the shawl peddler opens up a sampler. The white silk of the samplers has turned ivory, and the embroidered flowers look as though they have been printed; time has pressed the threads into the fabric. Anyway, we know the pieces are at least a hundred years old, passed from father to son, because the needlework is too painstaking to be made by contemporary human hands. Luminescent silk threads embroidered on the jaded cloth glow like uncut rubies, emeralds, pearls, and diamonds in antique jewelry. The samplers are embroidered with myriad flowers representing an infinite number of possibilities, and they are the birthplace of generations of shawls. The same motifs are chosen, as in life, and arranged and rearranged again and again to create entirely new universes.

The women take in the palette that has been presented to them on the sampler. They are soon engrossed in mixing and matching, choosing and designing. I, a small observer, sitting on the broad ledge of the window where the light is excellent, copy the shapes of the flowers and the leaves on white letter paper that I will later fill in at school, which is where I keep all my art materials. The paper and pencil accompany me almost everywhere I go.

It is an afternoon of beauty and art. The women know that the shawl maker is listening intently and will faithfully execute their masterpieces. When the finished shawls come back the women delight in one another's work and bemoan their own choice or their luck in the embroidery apprentice who falls to their lot.

⚘⚘⚘

The shawl maker is a dandy. He wears kohl in his eyes, and his hair under his curly, lamb fetus–fur hat is copper red from henna dye. He always seems to have saliva in his mouth, and though it looks as if he's holding it back by cupping his lower lip, it's just his enthusiasm for his wares. He has puzzles and nonsense rhymes, with which he entertains himself and us children while the women look at his shawls.

"I have a daughter who is smarter than my sons," he says to me one day. "Izmat is her name and she is as old as you. I will bring her the next time I come by."

The shawl man has named his daughter with the word meaning honor and she must have been born, like me, in a year of tumult. It is a good name, we live among each other by honor, we do not have dependable, government-controlled credit agencies or welfare systems. He keeps his word and brings Izmat a month or so later, and as he had said she is my age. She looks like a perfect little lady with a round face and soft brown eyes. Her hair is parted in the middle and braided in two plaits which come down on either side of the front of her little tweed *pheran*. I don't know it then, but she will part her hair in the middle for the rest of her life, changing only from braids to a clip with a single pony tail when she grows up. Izmat joins us in her father's rhyming games.

For one game he gently pounds our lower jaw up against the upper jaw with his closed fist while we repeat a nonsense rhyme. The object is to catch our tongue between our teeth.

"Ten teeth chattering, ten tongues running. Ten tuck tuck tucks," the shawl man says as we fall into the game and repeat the rhyme while trying to save our tongues.

The women laugh when we pronounce words in the rhyme the way he does, like a Muslim, although the words are exactly the same for Hindus. He loves to make us all laugh with sales talk in English employed in the past for British memsahibs, "Antique piece. Moghul princess. Paisley motif. English rose. Very fine. Uncommon piece. Lovely."

He sits with us and sips his tea, but his ear is cocked toward the women. Whenever a question arises about his shawls he shouts back an answer at the women, and looks at them from the corner of his eye to gauge the body language of purchase.

Sometimes he forgets himself and something comes over his eyes and he puts his hand behind his head and pushes his hat forward at a rakish angle. It is a momentary lapse and he immediately rectifies the slip by making as if he has to scratch his head and places his unborn lamb's-fur hat squarely on his head again.

It is a family gathering and he is part of it, it is a time for tea and gossip. Frequent visits to a home with a young girl can mean only one thing, trousseau preparation, and he, an intrinsic part of it, relishes the secrecy and the profit.

In a universe of joint and extended families something is always about to happen. Young women and men are always coming of age and shifting the kaleidoscope into acceptable or difficult configurations. It is all grist for his mill. If it goes smoothly then there is a marriage and money for him, and if not it is whispered, discreet gossip, which is his stock in trade as well, a little bonus thrown in only for his long-standing clientele.

Usually, though, one cousin comes of age, then another, then another, and pashmina is required for all of them and their spouses, or the master of the house may suddenly feel like a brand-new pashmina shawl-blanket. The shawl peddler is a busy man and causes great consternation by not showing up on a promised day. If he is late, even by hours, we don't mind. We have a different take on punctuality, and often say "The more delayed you are, the better you arrive." Time always adds value. When he does show up he spends a good part of the morning or the afternoon with us. After a few hours of selection and chatter, the shawl session ends, and the shawl man carefully folds up and puts away his silk archives and then his shawls.

More often than not one of us ends up requesting a paisley pattern. We consider the paisley, dancing among other designs like a self-assured languid beauty, the symbol of timeless perfection. There is hardly a woman in Kashmir who does not have something with the familiar paisley embroidered on it. We call it an "almond" because that is what we grow while the people from the hot plains of India call it a "little mango" because that is their fruit.

We don't know much about mangoes and we hardly ever see any except for a brief period in the summer when a few survive our icy mountain passes and arrive at our fruit markets. Like lemons, bananas, and oranges, mangoes are very exotic to us and we have to import them. Our fruits are apples, peaches, cherries, apricots, plums, pears, melons, almonds, walnuts, and grapes. Even the flowers in Kashmir are different: we have narcissus, lotus, tulips, wild roses, hyacinths, peonies, irises, lilies. Our trees are Himalayan, and of course we cannot say it often enough, in all of India only we have the chinar. The other most requested embroidery from the sampler is the leaf of the chinar tree.

The chinar was bequeathed to us by the Mughal emperors, who imported it from Persia. The "on fire tree" which is how the chinar looks in the fall, is more than a tree. It is a historical legacy protected by law and you may not cut it down even if it grows in your own backyard. We treat it as if it is a benevolent old lady, we sleep the sweetest sleep in its shade, and some women are given its Kashmiri name, which is *booyne*. The chinar leaves take us from season to season, going from pale green buds in spring to large leaves in summer's full green, to flame red, retreating into brown and then into nothingness. When the chinar leaves are done in the fall we gather them from the ground to burn them for our winter coals. Our autumn air is redolent with the smoke from piles of burning chinar leaves and twigs, the very scent of home as I remember it, decades later. The winter in Kashmir takes up almost half the year.

Winter is eventually done, but the air, remembering the durable season, is still clear and cold. Then the ice gives way to snow, and the snow gives way here and there to brown earth and wisps of new green grass. Slowly and surely the sun starts gaining the upper hand. Spring is not quite here in full bloom, but the narcissus appears, eyes closed, and then suddenly opens up one day laden with fragrance. We cut a couple of the flowers and place them in a vase inside the house and live on its fragrance until spring bursts upon us fully a few weeks later. Our flowers are in our soil, and in the few houses that still have mud-thatched roofs our soil sends up wild relatives of these floral natives.

Once spring comes, the narcissus is no longer queen and disappears silently in obeisance to apple, almond, cherry, and peach blossoms. We almost run out of our houses with picnic baskets and children and mothers-in-law and new brides, and kangris and samovars, and find our way to the orchards by boat and bus and horse-driven carriage. It is a madness of perfumed air, outdoor Kashmiris, and the promise of fruits and flowers in our lanes and countryside.

The shawl maker has all these symbols of our life firmly catalogued in fine stitches on his cherished samplers. Occasionally, lost among Kashmiri motifs, one finds a very English-looking rose, no doubt requested by a homesick memsahib, and now immortalized in the frieze.

In spite of the shawl peddler's protestations, no one does that kind of fine work anymore. The old masters are too old and the young would rather make money quickly. But the shawl seller swears that the samplers are the standard to which he adheres.

"This is why you open your doors to me when I knock. Otherwise every other person in Kashmir is a shawl maker," he says, looking us right in the eye.

He tries hard, of course, but times have changed. In the past artists were said to have gone blind bringing the Mughal Gardens in silk to a half-blind Sikh emperor who could not travel to Kashmir. When the carpets were unraveled before him the emperor took off his shoes so that he could walk in the gardens of Kashmir. His bejeweled ladies wept as they wore the embroidered shawls they were presented because they had no idea that such beautiful flowers or such gossamer wool existed in this world.

No one was going blind with universal adult suffrage in full force now, but still the standard was good to have. You could not stray too far from it. There were great-grandmothers in many houses who remembered how things were done.

When the shawls are delivered and carefully opened it is difficult to imagine that it is the coarse knotted hands of men with gray and white stubble that have embroidered such sophisticated patterns. The stitches are hardly visible to the naked eye, and so meticulous that there is no right side, they nestle in the pashmina and are lost in it. Only the art remains to allure us. Like the emperor and his women, the women of my home dance in their flower garden, exulting in the execution of their patterns and arrangements.

The masters are all older men. Nimbler apprentice hands fill in routine edges and borders, all repetitive work. This is the groundwork for their mastering the art. They serve their teachers many years with this humility before they themselves turn gray and proficient. Then a new crop of apprentices brings the teachers tea, or fills their chillum with tobacco, and topping the tobacco with tiny chinar coals, lights their hookah. This is the natural order of things, but it is well known that one never knows what to expect of a new crop.

Occasionally a genius emerges among the apprentices and the shawl man proudly shows off his prodigy, then warily watches him flourish and then sourly and quietly acknowledges that the fellow has gone off with someone else, forgetting that it was he who taught him everything.

Our shawl maker, whose family has had most of our family business for generations, has a shop deep in the entrails of Srinagar. His workshop is in an alcove above the showroom. We cannot see the workers, but we can hear the rumble of the hookah, we can also smell the incense they burn to counter the smell of tobacco smoke. We can hear the sewing machine upstairs and soft laughter or conversation among the apprentices. It is a man's world up there, and all the men are busy working on the most subtle embroidery possible. The proprietor descends the narrow staircase coming down from the alcove and takes his place behind the wooden counter to discuss business with us. Nothing is ever ready on time, and it is understood that we have to make a few fruitless visits to the shop before the work is completed and handed to us. As an apology he offers us hot green tea laced with fragrant nuts and spices, but we politely refuse. Neither will he ever give us anything on time, nor will we stop going to his shop. It is part of the whole transaction.

We visit the old city very infrequently; we are too used to the wide streets and modern transportation of suburban life. We enter the labyrinth of the old city only when we visit our relatives, who still live in intricately carved and delicately bricked ancestral homes, or when we attend weddings or family functions. On these occasions we go in a small one-horse *tanga* for most of the way, perhaps walking the last hundred yards or so of cobbled mazelike narrow lanes on foot. If the celebrations go on late into the night and we cannot find a tanga to come back in we just walk home, singing loudly at the midnight moon, with a chaperone or a servant in tow. Invariably we are joined in our walk and our serenade by stray dogs, of which there is never a shortage in the streets of Srinagar.

The houses in the old city, Muslim and Hindu houses, are sometimes so close together that the owners can pass things to each other from the windows. Everyone knows everyone and their business, and the housewives share domestic woes and gossip, talking loudly across windows.

Women take a careful look down into the street before throwing out the boiling-hot starch water they have to drain out every day from the cooked rice. If her neighbor is doing the same, it is impossible that the two women will go back to their chores before bringing each other up to date on their domestic goings-on. Of one thing one can be sure, it will not be good news. We never announce good news because we are obsessed with the evil eye, which according to many has reduced entire mountains to dust. Whenever anyone asks us how we are doing we look as though we are recovering from something, no one wants to look prosperous or well. We are not comfortable with prosperity and well-being, having seen it at close quarters only for a short while. Having given us the most beautiful place in the world to live in God has evened the score by alternately subjecting us to serfdom and embattlement with the forces of nature on a regular basis. Our history has been under the joint custody of oppressive rulers and an earthly trinity of earthquakes, famine, and floods. These are etched into our genes and we never forget, even at the best of times.

No wonder, then, that parents want to do the best they can to ensure that their child is warm and never in need of cash. This is why the shawl man and the jeweler are so critical to wedding preparations. When the house is in the grip of marriage fever, our favorite catharsis, the shawl man also becomes a victim of the malady. After the girl of the house gets married he follows her to her new address. If he already knows the people there, he is also the most reliable informant about the goings on at her in-laws' home. Sometimes he carries camouflaged messages back and forth. And, when lives move ahead and scenes shift, it is to the same shawl man that a young woman might sell the first half of her pashmina sari. She never forgets what my grandmother also wants me to remember always, that pashmina is currency. If the bad times continue she will sell the other half as well. If so instructed, he will not tell her parents about these transactions.

"What sort of bad times?" I ask Dhanna.

High above my grandmother's head pictures of our gods and goddesses hang in the ceiling cornice. Mostly the pictures are of our favorite, the Mother-Goddess known by her many names: Durga, Ragnya, Sharika, Bhawani. She sits sidesaddle or astride a demure tiger, her several arms hold everything vital to a good life. She Who Fears Nothing dismounts only to destroy evil wherever it hides its ugly self. In one of the pictures hanging above our heads in Dhanna's kitchen hall She, bloody sword in hand, has her feet planted firmly atop the Demon Bull, while her tiger playfully gambols with the severed Demon Head. She is our Mother and she is the embodiment of Positive Energy. I look up at the pictures, and wonder. We have grown up with Tiger Ladies all around us, even our men are in mortal terror of them, and make pilgrimages and pray to them constantly. Our goddess is invincible, and we take that for granted. I cannot imagine what a woman could suffer without her parents and siblings knowing about it.

"Well, she had no income, she was shy and could not ask her

husband or her in-laws for money if she needed it for something. She hardly knows them," answers my grandmother.

My eyes scroll down from the Tiger Ladies to her. I ask her, hoping for a fresh detail, but I know the answer. I know from looking around me that things have changed for the better for daughters-in-law, but not completely, and there are some stubborn pockets of resistance in my family as well.

For the in-laws the bride is a new thing, an unknown entity, someone who will eventually, with luck and perseverance, be accorded her place in their scheme of things. For now she is much younger than the other women, smells too much of bridal finery and perfumed oils. Who knows what she knows or what she can do? She is an outsider who shares the son's bed, she is suspect, and soon provides proof of her nocturnal antics in the shape of an oval belly. The belly will become her passport to the family. The fact is that even producing an offspring who is a blood relative of her in-laws does not guarantee that she will become a real member of the pack.

The misery of daughters-in-law is a theme we are all familiar with. Our folk songs, folktales, and mythology are full of the laments of young girls torn from their parents and hurled into new unforgiving households. Sometimes the girl's wet nurse or chaperone, whom we call milk-mother, goes to look her up, as her own parents are not supposed to set foot in the in-laws' house. If the girl is too homesick or she has to return to her parents' house for a ritual, or because of an illness, the milk-mother will bring her back for a brief visit. If the girl is a really young child bride, not yet partner in her young husband's bed, the milk-mother will bring her back more often, carrying her on her shoulders, completely covered with a shawl so that her gold jewelry does not attract attention. When the little girl reaches her parents she is relieved of her burdensome ornaments and goes out to play with her siblings and cousins. But she belongs to another house now.

We sing the songs of these unhappy brides even at weddings, and narrate heartrending tales that bring tears even to the eyes of the driest of mothers-in-law, because they have been brides themselves. Even our Sufi mystics and poetesses are not free from this tribulation. One story we know particularly well because the mystic is a woman from our ancestral family. Generations later her prophecies are alarmingly potent and we are scrupulously observant of her special days. I know what my grandmother means when she says "Sometimes new brides have to face tough times at the hands of their in-laws."

"Or," says my grandmother, watching me carefully, "if a woman was ill, or anyone else was ill, and they could not cure the illness with herbs and poultices, and had no choice but to buy medicines. People did not have big jobs in those days. They had rice and greens, and yogurt if they were lucky, but not much money. If one was lucky one person in the family had a job and he supported everyone, things were cheap then, living was simple. Everyone lived under the same roof, in a joint family. We were clothed in white."

In an era where virtually all the employment came from a feudal colonial government, she means we belonged to a painfully respectable middle class who had to wear clean, starched-white clothes to their British Indian offices. Wearing colorful clothes to work indicated flamboyance in the face of capricious authority, a dangerous idea. People considered themselves extremely fortunate to have even the smallest office job in the remotest branch of the government. The upper class barely lived comfortably, and the rich you could count on one hand. Now, it is after independence, and most people are still poor, but we natives are employed from top to bottom, in every kind of job, everywhere.

I am at an age where I cannot bear the truth. These stories about sick women and apathetic in-laws depress me and my grandmother can see it in my eyes. She flips over the trout to crisp it on the other side. Normally she cuts the trout into appropriate pieces, but for me she has chosen a small fish and is frying it in its entirety, a special treat. She sees my face and becomes a comedian for my sake.

"Women are really clever," she says. "They know what to do. They roasted eggs in their kangris under their clothes."

Women are inseparable from their kangris, they carry the perpetual fire between their breasts, next to their womb, and between their loins. They cannot afford to let the fire die, and they keep an eye on it all the time. At weddings and special occasions married girls are given kangris by their parents. It is yet another essential item in a daughter's survival kit. But these gift kangris are more festive than everyday ones and even have colored silver paper slipped in between the wicker and the terra-cotta pot as the basket is woven. The latticed silver paper shimmers as the pot is carried by hand. A beautifully filigreed stoker made of sterling silver is tied to the back of the basket and this final touch completes the gift. The functionality of the stoker is limited; it will soften and bend if used seriously, so it is soon replaced with an iron one. The silver, inexorably, like other insurance policies, joins the pashmina and the bitter flowers in a secret treasure chest.

"Eggs in their kangris?" I ask, quite delighted by the thought of women egg bandits. I decide that I shall roast eggs in my kangri very soon.

My grandmother is happy to see that she has made me smile. She continues, refueled. "The women stole into the chicken coop, picked up an egg or two, and placed it under the hot ash in their kangris. Then, carrying it under their pheran with one hand, they would go out into the garden, or the backyard, or the riverbank, or their own room. Then they might fish out the egg with the stoker and have a nice little snack, without bothering the kitchen or, best of all, without anyone knowing. No one looked after the women; they were supposed to look after everyone and, of course, no one ever asked if they were hungry." She smiles conspiratorially at me, another woman in the making.

The egg women are radical compared to Dhanna. My grandmother does not eat eggs or fowl, because they are unclean. She will not allow either to be cooked in her kitchen; she looks indignant even when fowl is cooked outside in the hall. There is no question of her touching fowl herself, and when it is brought into the house she walks around looking self-righteous all the while. She doesn't like the idea and she doesn't like the smell. On the other hand, lamb and fish have direct access to the kitchen and are sometimes cooked even for religious occasions. Garlic, shallots, and onions, sensual bulbs all, and openly bloody tomatoes, are also outcasts from her kitchen, just like fowl. If a bulb does not send up flowers she has no use for it. It all seems so logical.

Then she remembers something. "One day my aunt nearly died of fright. She was a sour old woman who could curdle a lot of milk. She terrified her new daughter-in-law silly with her sarcasm and anger."

I am given facial expressions and body language to illustrate the point.

"The young woman sat next to auntie on the carpet, head bowed down, firepot under her bent knees under her pheran, as it should be, and all was quiet. Suddenly a bomb exploded. The old woman ran out of the room screaming, and fell out of the balcony. Thank God it was only the first floor. When all was quiet they found the young one with ash all over her face and egg and eggshell splattered everywhere. The egg in her firepot had exploded and risen with all its volcanic ash up her shirt collar and into her nose and hair. She looked so much like a wandering ascetic that everyone was a bit wary of her after that."

We have a special regard for people who have ash smeared all over their face and body.

"Now all the young women wear saris," says my grandmother. She is somewhat contemptuous of non-Kashmiri imported couture. She is proud of her pheran, a voluminous ankle-length caftan with huge sleeves worn over a long cotton shell, the traditional dress of Kashmiri women and men. The sleeves are so wide that in the winter the arms stay inside the wool pheran, coming out only when absolutely required to do so.

The pheran can cover a lot of things. The last refuge of cold and tired grandchildren, it is loose enough to hold one adult and one child, and the neck is deep enough for the child's head to pop out from under the grandparent's chin, like a baby kangaroo. Of course, there is always a place for a kangri as well.

My grandmother gives me a second helping of my favorite meal of crisply fried trout, untouchably hot, garnished with salt and red pepper, and mixed with cold, sweet leftover rice. I eat heavenly morsels of the juxtaposition of the hot and the cold. As I eat, my grandmother watches me intensely. She involuntarily copies my facial motions of mastication: one person is eating but two are being fed.

Years later my daughter will ask for an encore of the same fish-rice combination. I will not say anything, but feel overjoyed when I see four generations of women with the same taste buds in one single dish.

After lunch my grandmother and I sit outside in the sun, which is so wonderful and bright that we have to shade our eyes with our hands. I squint at Dhanna and ponder the fact that the only friend a woman has in her married state is her yardage of pashmina cloth. My grandmother interrupts my thoughts to say, "Fathers also gave their daughters wedding ear ornaments to make sure they had extra gold in case they needed it." Only married pandit women wear solid gold earrings, symbols of married status called *dejahor*, which hang all the way down to their nipples.

"When women needed money, or when their daughters got married, they would cut off one dejahor, sell it, and make two of the other one. The size was the same, but it was hollow inside and no one would know that they had troubles. You always have to have two, one for each ear." She tells me again and again to make sure I know that balance is critical.

I lean forward and lift the heavy gold pendants she is wearing, and now they look like mini-banks to me. She has not had to replace hers with hollow ones because she did not need the money like so many others. In her house it was her husband's solid gold medal for his master's degree in economics from Lahore University that was melted down for the ornaments. The fact that he stood first was enough—they knew it and everyone else knew it—and besides, who was going to wear such a large medal anyway? Now, the gold sovereign with beautiful Queen Victoria is a different story. She has several of those, and she has strung them in gold necklaces she has designed for her children.

Her wedding ornaments have ornaments of their own, a gold toothpick, a miniature spoon-shaped ear cleanser, and other little utensils; it is a twenty-four-karat gold Swiss knife of sorts. Over the years her collection of little gold gadgets has been attached piece by piece like charms to her breast-length wedding earrings. After meals she uses the toothpick casually; its constant presence on her breast has immunized her to its value.

Dhanna knows very little of what is going on beyond her immediate neighborhood. For her, Lahore University is still where everyone goes to study, where her husband was given the heavy round gold medal. She knows that something called Pakistan has happened, but grand old Lahore has nothing to do with it. She comes to know about Pakistan when her daughter is pregnant with me, and nightmarish stories related by fleeing families from our outlying villages bring everything to a standstill in Kashmir.

ﬞ ﬞ ﬞ

It is 1947. Outside the valley in India, nothing stays in place as churning lines of humanity run hither and yon in a hellish frenzy, trying to find their way. India has just been sliced in two, and both parts are quivering like newly slaughtered flesh. Parts of the country are being apportioned as if at a sacrificial ritual, presided over by the high priests of our national dismemberment, the departing British government. At the height of the madness, to precipitate its acquisition of Kashmir, Pakistan sends Afghan hill tribes called Kabailis to invade Kashmir. The tribesmen's appetites are whetted by truckloads of carpets, brassware, and luxury goods borrowed from wealthy homes, topped by a beautiful prostitute, borrowed from her usual chores, and sometimes a fresh corpse borrowed from the morgue. They are told that all this had been easily looted from Kashmir, and that the brassware is pure gold, and that this is what they will find once they reach Kashmir. These tribesmen are intrepid warriors but not connoisseurs of the fine life. The trucks look good enough to them and soon they are on their way, hungry, pouring into the valley, guns on their shoulders, ready for the kill.

As the Kabailis come down into the valley they see a Kashmiri shepherd and ask him directions to Srinagar, the capital of Kashmir, where we live. One look at their guns and knives tells him they do not belong in the valley and he sends them in the opposite direction. When they discover what he has done, they return, track him down, and crucify him with nails driven through his hands and heart and head at the very crossroads where he misled them.

In our part of the world, land disputes abound, and petty thievery, but our thieves are so petty that they are objects of humorous folklore. Murder or serious robbery is almost unheard of, and this unspeakable act and the shepherd's martyrdom are never forgotten. My grandmother, the midnight bather, is beside herself with anxiety for her first grandchild, yet to be born.

"Who are these people? What did we do to them, why have

they come?" She is told that Pakistan has sent the raiders to Kashmir. The raiders have come hunting infidels and treasures and beautiful women. The women of Kashmir are beautiful, the songs from Persia to China have said for centuries, but it is soon apparent that neither religion nor beauty is what the men are after. If you come in their way, whatever your beliefs or looks, they dispatch you with the same fierceness with which they tore the British army to shreds a century ago, reducing entire battalions to just a shattered man or two.

The Kabailis are approaching us fast and are only about three hours away in the foothills of the mountains. People flee in the opposite direction, taking just a few possessions. My family also runs, to a Muslim friend's house where we are quickly hidden in the women's quarters.

We all live on food given us by our Muslim friends; no one asks who cooked it. As we wait for the outcome of the attack, we can hardly breathe because the hordes have left behind sickening acts of cruelty. Even our hosts are not safe if they harbor us, but to them the choice is simple and made immediately. They sit protectively in their outer rooms. They are one of the few families with a telephone, but phones are out of commission so they sit glued to the radio for news of the fighting. Then the raiders attack the power station and we are surrounded by an awful silence. I am in my mother's belly, and she is also hiding in the dark, waiting for deliverance with the rest of my family.

జజజ

Help arrives in time in planeloads of the Indian army. The Kabailis are sent back without any carpets, infidels, or beautiful women, but they do manage to extricate an odd gold tooth or two pulled out of the mouths of some hapless Irish nuns they attack at a rural outpost of the order. The Mother Superior and her nuns had tried to smile at the tribesmen, hoping to stir some humanity in their cartridge belt–decorated chests. By the time the tribesmen's stop at the convent was over, one nun lay dead, savagely murdered in cold blood. But they managed to save the girls at the convent school, it was said.

ッッッ

We went home in a few days when the worst was over, after the intruders had been rounded up and sent back. A couple of the Kabailis had managed to reach Srinagar, though, and we watched with terror and relief as one, twice the height and width of his captors, was marched down our main road on the way to the police station.

Now the word "Pakistan" is initiated into my grandmother's vocabulary. Even so, the geography and the history of our world are too ancient to be changed in our hearts so quickly. It will take decades for us to redo our inner maps. Now Lahore is the heart of Pakistan, but for those who knew her when everyone was an Indian there is no other city. My grandmother thinks her husband will always buy her shoes from Lahore's Anarkali Bazaar, the only place in the world where the suede is soft enough for her feet.

The assault has made us aware that to outsiders we are not Kashmiris but Hindus. There is no question of Kashmiris betraying other Kashmiris to some wild mountain people just because we are Hindus and they are Muslims. Our language and culture has bound us Kashmiris so strongly together that all other people, regardless of religion, are strangers to us. If someone does not understand our language, our stories, our songs, and our food, they are foreigners to us. This rule of the valley applies to our royal family as well. Our rulers are from a different culture and do not speak our language.

The monarchs of Kashmir have almost always been foreigners who have treated native Kashmiris, Hindus and Muslims, like serfs. In fact, the words "work" and "exploitation" are jokingly, but very often, used interchangeably. The Muslim rulers of Kashmir were succeeded by the Sikhs, who were followed by a Hindu dynasty of the Dogras, a warrior caste from Jammu, a kingdom just outside the valley, where the great hot plains of north India begin.

Kashmir was a thank-you present given to our Dogra rulers by the British in the nineteenth century. Ever reluctant to forgo territorial gains the British stationed a Resident in our state of Jammu and Kashmir to keep a close eye on matters. Now, in 1947, the British are beating a hasty retreat, but we do not achieve independence like the rest of India because our Maharajah is dragging his feet all over his hillside palace. The ruler of Kashmir does not want to exchange his mountain kingdom for a republic.

For all of us there is ultimately a time of reckoning, and we are usually hauled to it by our own actions. The tribesmen close in on the valley and our king has to make a move. As we Kashmiris wait tremulously for him to take charge he takes off for the airport and requisitions an aircraft that flies him to his ancestral capital, Jammu. Eventually he will go to his favorite playground, Bombay, never to return. The Maharajah's abdication leaves us to our own devices. Now everything is in the hands of a Kashmiri Muslim political leader. We call Sheikh Abdullah "The Tiger of Kashmir." The Tiger does not really care for Pakistan and joins free India.

We now have an indigenous head of government for the first time in centuries. But Sheikh Abdullah is more than just that, he is a folk hero who has delivered his valley from the tribesmen of Pakistan by calling in the Indian army. In a few short tumultuous days we have nonviolently replaced our monarchy with a democracy, we have our own popular leader, and we are now part of the Republic of India.

We do not want to become a gift again. A Kashmiri pandit,

Jawahar Lal Nehru is the Prime Minister of India. Nehru and the Kashmiri leaders agree that the accession will eventually be formalized by a people's poll. We are no longer the oppressed, now we are a democracy and we must be consulted. We were hardly aware that while we Kashmiris were awaiting rescue and running to help one another, India was torn apart at the chest. Murdered Hindus and Muslims, torn limbs and souls, and burning houses lie scattered all over. Though we are surrounded by religious strife our shared life in the valley keeps us Kashmiris together. We revel in one another's mysteries and legends and re-sort to them when required, which is frequently. One of the legends that we hold in common is that of the repeated resurrection of Kashmir from the annihilations it has suffered through its history.

"Once in ancient times there were only eleven families left in Kashmir. Now look, everyone is home!" our elders tell us, when we despair about any impossible situation.

This tells us that once you have faced the impossible, only the possible remains.

It is a reassuring myth, and we seem to need to hear it.

My family returns home after the confusion and terror of the *raid,* as we call it. They open up the windows and air the house, dust and clean the furniture, light the kitchen fires and settle back into their routines. Everyone is unsteady after the brief exodus, and probably as a result of the dislocation my mother gives birth to me a few weeks earlier than expected.

Dhanna is taken unawares by my mother's sudden onset of labor. If she knew I would suddenly appear that particular day she would have done everything to hasten or delay labor. She loves me the minute I am born, but horoscopes have already been consulted and for a while during my mother's labor, it looks as if I might appear at an hour considered unlucky for my family.

The astrologer says, "If the child is born before midnight it will never live with you."

This pronouncement is taken to mean that birth at an inauspicious hour will cause harm to either the child or the family. Something has to be done and the astrologer suggests adoption. My grandmother says she will adopt me and give me her name because it is different from my mother's married name. She is suggesting a common remedy in a superstitious valley, using nominal jugglery to trick fate. We firmly believe that forging the identity of the newborn, who does not come with a name tag, can work wonders.

My mother's mother can only offer her thoughts on the subject, in a whisper to my other grandmother. After all, like my mother I belong to my father's house.

My father's family does not believe in all this nonsense but puts up with Dhanna because they are all a bit in awe of her. My father is still a student and neither of my parents is yet twenty years old, so in any case my mother and I shall be staying with my paternal grandparents.

Fortunately, though, the labor is delayed and I am born at the right time, late, and safely past the perilous hour. The joy of a safe delivery after a dark and frightening time provides anecdotes for years afterward.

New births, new configurations, and new preoccupations ensure that the tribesmen are put away in the recesses of our minds. The valley picks up where it left off. Relieved of the feudal trappings of our monarchy, we resume our lives in our new world with some significant changes. Muslims come into prominence everywhere, rapidly gaining control of jobs in proportion to their vast numbers in Kashmir. Hindus continue as before and Grandpa Babuji, a Hindu, is the Home Secretary. Most Kashmiris being Muslim, Islamic precepts and traditions flourish along with Hinduism. This does not change anything between us Hindus and Muslims, we have always known and respected each other's beliefs. Kashmiri Hindus have had trouble only from outsiders, never from other Kashmiris.

Both religious communities have happily made amendments to their own taboos and our lives are harmoniously mingled. We quietly pass each other coveted dishes, forbidden in traditional interaction, over the backyard fence. We attend each other's weddings with pleasure and enjoyment. On the night that henna is applied to the groom or the bride, we stay up all night singing songs, sipping green tea with crushed cardamom, cinnamon, and almonds. If we are lucky, the tea will also be flavored with saffron; one sip and we imbibe the souls of a thousand crocus flowers. On these nights, in our gardens, under red and yellow and green awnings designed in Mughal times our songs and love stories are the same.

We sing the songs of a beautiful village girl in a field of purple flowers. She is gathering crocus for saffron, singing her poems of yearning and love. Habba Khotoon is oblivious to a prince passing by on his way to a hunting trip; he is the namesake of a certain Joseph of an earlier time, and like him enticing in his beauty. Yusuf Shah Chak has stopped in his tracks and cannot bear to go home without Habba Khotoon, but she is already married to a village boy. Her lips are on fire from her songs and her saffron and he is consumed. For the first time someone is captivated by Habba Khotoon's poems and cannot live without them. She is easily persuaded and leaves the village to become the adored poet-queen of King Yusuf. But time never moves forward in a straight line; it lives in cycles and what begins must end. Royal duties separate the lovers, and Habba Khotoon's agonized messages for Yusuf, tall and dazzling like a blossoming tree, reverberate in our gatherings three hundred years later. She lives forever as a pioneer of love poetry in Kashmir, and Yusuf lives with her as the object of her desire.

Our love is more cautious, and even though we Hindus and Muslims share a passion for our Kashmiri lives, we are careful not to tread on each other's toes. Although we attend each other's weddings intermarriage is inconceivable, and you can count such events on the tips of the fingers of one hand, if you care to. Mostly we just ignore such violations of our taboos, even though in our chronicled past our kings and queens married in and out of their religion when it was politically expedient. Now our mutual acceptance of our established customs makes a good fence and we are exemplary neighbors.

In any event, the valley cradles us in her beauty and love songs, and does not leave us with much time or desire to hate anything. Visitors to the valley call us lazy, and the Western-educated among us call themselves the Lotus-Eaters, but we live in heaven. Kashmiris pray to long-gone Sufi mystics, madwomen and madmen who are our poets and prophets. Our Sufism is a combination of the esoteric elements of Hinduism and Islam, and gives the highest priority to what-is-not-of-this-world. With us reason is not everything, and insanity demands instant veneration. We stand timorously at attention should a mad person enter our home. We make way for them, for they are the last symbols of our Sufi past. Our literature is the legacy of these prolific men and women of "flashing eyes and floating hair."

We listen carefully to what the men and women of the world of nonreason say. We try to divine meanings out of lunatic acts like throwing flowers at passers-by or spitting at a host, or standing in the courtyard warning of unseemly or wonderful things. Powerful men and women gratefully take little "prescriptions" written by a "doctor" in tatters, with mucus dripping from his nose into his mouth and matted beard. We cherish this mimicry of pen and paper, and gratefully receive crumpled scribbles from our wild-eyed visitors. We hold these talismans dear to our hearts and well-being. Stories of miracles and prophecy are circulated with equal conviction among housewives, physicists, boatmen, and professors of English. A fine chaos of reason prevails; it is all a part of our nature and in the very water we drink.

The folly of not acknowledging seers and mystics is known only too well to us. In particular it is the women mystics who rule our minds and hearts, calling us like sirens with their mystical songs and lamentations. These poetesses are part of our long literary tradition, and of our folklore and mythology. We repeatedly hear stories about them, but it is the singing of their verses in our homes that binds us to our mystics.

We are steeped in complete faith because every day we see the verses of our saints come true.

"It had started off badly." The women tell us the story of one of our oracular women. "He could never shut the bedroom door completely, in case his mother called for water or God knows what."

We know the story in detail by now. When the man and woman are alone, he makes sure the room is darkened, the windows shut, the curtains drawn, doors bolted, as if he is aware of an interloper, as if he is ashamed of being a married man. All possible entrances are secured except the one leading to his mother's bedroom. In silence he makes love to his wife, one hand on her mouth, and he consumes her with hunger. But he is like a man under siege, a man pursued. In the night he looks at her and is possessed by her luminescence and her hair and her nakedness. When morning comes and he draws the curtains from the windowpanes and opens all the windows and doors he has closed the night before, he can see her teeth and her nakedness stretched across the bed. He hears his mother calling him, and when he remembers his need in the night it makes his stomach turn.

Then he has a great urge to flee and free himself. So, he makes some derogatory remarks and snips off all the ephemeral threads of the night. She goes about her work, a complete woman, and she forgives his dilemma and his incompleteness. During the day they work like functionaries in an establishment, each has their own routine to attend to. It is as if they do not know each other, and they do not exchange a word unless it is absolutely essential. During the day he ministers to his mother completely, no divided loyalties, a free man. Only then, at night, hiding in the dark, can he feel free to be with his wife.

The time comes for him to choose between right and wrong, but his mind is locked and he is not free. He has to give up one for the other. In the absence of wisdom he is guided solely by destiny and he makes his thoughtless choice.

He slides under his mother's quilt; it has lilacs and ferns printed on it. But that was a long time ago; and you can barely make out the lilacs now. Her bony knees are tucked up under her leathery wizened breast. Her eyes are small, glutinous, flat and open like a fish. She does not ask, but he has come to some conclusions and is more or less ready with a verdict.

"Her nipples are small, and she has hair on her face," he says.

His mother makes a short wheezing sound which signifies that she has known it all along.

"And that is not all, her head seems to be on fire all the time. And if I tell you something you will not believe me. One night she thought I was sleeping and she summoned a tiger from the wooden ceiling and rode off into the night."

The old woman lets out a quick gasp and her knuckles turn white as she tries to sit upright.

"I have heard of such things," she says with fear in her voice. She thinks she knows the wretched truth, something she had a feeling about all along. The very son she sought to protect is sleeping with a demoness.

Things go from bad to worse. The son lingers more and more in the kitchen, where his mother spends all her time, eating tidbits and sipping tea. He tells his mother astonishing things.

"She rolls herself into a small ball that glows like mercury, and if I try to look at her she darts about the room and finally comes to rest only when I close my eyes and cover my head. I can't see but I know, just as I know that it is morning even before I open my eyes. I see the sky come down through the window into the room and she lets it in through her ring as she holds it between her thumb and forefinger. In the morning she goes about her business, milks the cows, feeds the birds and the plants, she goes down to the river to bathe, but she never leaves the room. She is there all the time, I know because she has a light around her, even in the dark, and it never leaves our room."

The mother listens and now she thinks she has to do something. He has let his mother into a sacred circle where she is forbidden. As a result everything is now dark and misleading to the old woman. Uncomprehending, she beats her breast silently, desperately, looking out at the mountains and up at the sky to see if they understand.

She whispers to her son, "A witch. What are we to do now?" They are mother and son again, united against the unknown.

The mother had anticipated that a daughter-in-law would cause dissonance in their perfect dead father–mother homestead. She pulls her quilt around her; she is overcome with dreadful certainty. Her blindness is about to wreak havoc upon them, but she cannot bring herself to make the right choice.

The lilacs on the quilt have faded, like lilacs in the spring, a brief interlude of heady perfume, like a passing woman on a busy street. The ferns are longer lasting; their green presence, albeit a bit patchy in places, pervades the quilt cover. The quilt is an old friend of the mother, together they were once robust, warm, colorful, and inviting, and together they have been respun and re-created from various disintegrations. In the summer the carders used to come, calling out in the streets, twanging their carding harps. Then the cotton was pulled out and aired and carded and fluffed up and restuffed into the quilt and restitched. In Kashmir you could afford to be without a quilt only for a couple of days in summer, the forests were as dense as ever and in the winter the snow covered everything.

When you could still see the lilacs spread in rich color among the deep green fanlike ferns on the quilt, she, a young woman then, slept soundly under it. Her lips were red from being chapped in the winter wind, her eyes heavy from sleep, her limbs tired from all that was required of them, her youthful face hidden under her black hair. On one such night, the moon, dressed as a thin curved knife, cut through the cold winter darkness while she slept as though death had borrowed her. Then she felt someone pull her long hair, which had fallen onto the wooden floor and her heart turned to ice. She sat up, but her husband tore her out of bed. She grasped the edge of the bed, and her quilt, but he pushed her down to the floor.

When she tried to resist, he dragged her across the floor and she pulled her quilt to cover her nakedness. He dragged her out of the room and threw her out on the landing outside. Then he went into their bedroom followed by a woman who closed the door behind them.

They said that after that the wife ran around town naked except for her stomach, which covered her because it had grown immense folds of lotus-like petals.

That is what some people said. But the woman with the lotus petals was someone else, a divine poet who wandered the valley, singing about the unity of all mankind, purifying and preparing herself for her union with God. It seems whenever people saw the mystic Lalleh Ded, all that was revealed to them was their own shame and nakedness, while she sang songs which covered the souls of the multitude that followed her with a permanent indigo dye.

This crone was neither that divine nor so lucky and her stomach had grown immense not from divine modesty but from the child she was carrying. She picked herself up, tended to her bruised knees and then to the infant at her breast, and she endured. The little creature looked up at her adoringly and held her finger tight, and she held on to him and cherished him beyond her dreams. She grew old in her husband's house, making herself useful as a scullery maid to her husband and his concubine. She brought up her only child, and together they watched her husband and his concubine die of the same disease.

Now the son is marriageable and his mother has her pride. Like mothers of all sons she sets out to find the best girl for her son, and she does. Once the bride, another woman's child, another young woman, has entered their portal she has to be fed, which is bad enough, but to nurture a sorceress? She watches her son at night as he follows his wife into the bedroom and closes the door behind him. The mother's blood has turned to venom, she cannot hold it within her. The girl has to be returned to her parents.

The old woman has to make sure that her son is not suffering from sexual nerves. Her son allows her to physically enter their living quarters, creeping in the door at night and hiding behind the great locked trunks of silver, silk, and pashmina the girl has brought in her trousseau. The daughter-in-law is the only daughter of a great sage, and he has given her everything.

"I knew her father had a lot to hide when I saw the trunks she brought," she had told her son. The old woman slides in behind the trunks and hides there.

When all is quiet and the son pretends to sleep the bride gets up from the bed, opens her hair, and, shaking it loose, lets it fall around her shoulders as she sits on the floor in the middle of the room. Her eyes are closed as she weaves her legs intricately. Very steadily a small circle of fire emanates from her head until a full column of flames shoots straight up from her head to the ceiling and through it upward to the heavens. The flames are of blinding white brilliance, but nothing catches fire as the column sweeps upward.

The mother-in-law, preoccupied all her life with only her own anatomical constrictions, vacuities, and denials, is blinded by what she has seen. She holds her hand to the wall; she has turned to stone, as it were. She comes to slowly but her brain is feverish now, the ideal place for destruction to germinate. The fire that has started there will burn everything down.

She tells herself, "My son is naive and practices no such meditations or austerities. He cannot stand up to this level of magic. She is not the proper wife for him. What shall I do, what shall I do now to protect him, is it too late?" She sits down in helplessness, wringing her hands. "Something has to be done."

But it is never too late for destruction. Next morning, still muttering under her breath, angry and sightless, armed with the necessary incomprehension she warily makes sarcastic remarks to the young woman. She hopes to provoke an outburst that will justify her actions. The son cowers in a corner of the kitchen.

"The marriage was Mother's idea," he says to himself. "So let her deal with it."

Their relatives sense that something is amiss and come in like predators sniffing a fresh kill, ready to tear the carcass apart still further.

The young woman is unperturbed. When she walks it looks as if there is an inch of space between her feet and the ground. She is serene in the face of all the ignorance around her, nothing else except God and her karma exist for her; it is as if she cannot hear or see anything else.

The next day she is gone.

The son looks for the light she used to leave behind, but his room is dark now, and empty. The room has become a space enclosed by walls, it is not even a place anymore. He knows then that he has heard her but he has not listened; he has looked at her but he has not seen her. He cries like a child, but his head is small and his mind has been nailed down too soon in his life and it cannot fly.

His mother consoles him. She says, "A man's heart is like a bird, it wants to sing on every branch. There are other branches, keep your heart within you."

The son looks at his mother vacantly. He does not tell her that his entire being has flown away and all she is looking at is his body. When he looks at his mother that is all he can see as well.

The old woman has scattered everything to the winds. The young woman has broken every tradition and returned to her father, who is her spiritual mentor as well. When he sent his daughter out into the world he had mixed oil and water, thinking he is just a father and she is just a daughter. Now she has come back to him to resume her meditations, purified of anything that might weigh her down.

The husband tosses and turns in his bed and looks out at the sky, which stays outside. He awakes with cold sweats at night and feels as though he is permanently in a cold hard desert. He refuses to come out of his room. In desperation his mother pleads with him and together they go to the girl's father's house to bring her back. But at her father's door they are told it is too late, and they are turned away.

The mother and son return to their home and live the rest of their dying lives in the blindness with which they covered their eyes.

We listen to these stories, which are told to us ad infinitum, and we know them in our heart and our head. Happily, none of these cautionary tales deter us from taking delight in, or being obsessed with, impending marriages. Neither are we intimidated. The most powerful mantra we know invokes Indrakshi, the fiercest form of the Tiger Lady, and it is passed from mother to daughter, but the men are careful with it as well. We know we have recourse and are never alone, and we always look upward and expect the best in forthcoming marriages. This is particularly true of grandmothers and mothers.

Dhanna and I are chasing the sun around the house, moving our chairs every half hour or so. Like other children in my family I call my grandparents by their names. She leans forward and feels the cartilage inside my upper earlobe, the area from which the wedding ornaments are going to be worn.

She says once again, "Your ears are ready for piercing; your mother must get it done now."

There is a note of pessimism in my grandmother's voice because she knows that if it was going to be done it would have been done much earlier, when the cartilage in the upper ear is as soft as it is in the lower lobe. She knows that my other grandfather's house is modern, and that I will probably never get my upper ears pierced; too many from my family have spent too many years in other parts of India where people live very different lives. She is filled with compassion for her poor daughter and granddaughter.

She says almost inaudibly, mainly to herself, "Where will you string your wedding ornaments if your upper ears are not ready? You cannot hang them over your ears like a horse."

She sees me as a smaller version of herself. She has had her Sikh jeweler with the intoxicated eyes fashion miniature versions of her gigantic gold wire hoops for me. I wear my child earrings in the unmarried part of my ear lobes, and she loves to see me wear the jewelry she orders for me.

"Look how pretty you look," she says, smiling proudly.

She holds my earrings between her thumb and forefinger and

gently pulls them, and me, close to her eyes as she checks the quality of the workmanship for the umpteenth time, but her thoughts are on my unpierced upper earlobes and my unpreparedness. She smiles at me as if I am deaf and dumb and have no idea of the foolishness of my modern parents.

Dhanna is known for her fierce temper, but I have never seen it. She is unafraid, particularly when it comes to protecting her children. She has great faith in her capabilities, and considers herself literate even though all she can do is sign her name as an organic whole, slowly, painstakingly in a childish hand on official documents. She who has won incredible battles with the logic of winter does not know the alphabet.

"Didn't you feel cold, bathing in the winter at the well?"

I think of the winter, which is protracted enough to have its own seasons of ice, which we call Old Man Chill, the Son Chill, and the Baby Chill. The Baby and the Old Man can freeze water dripping from rooftops into brilliant giant icicles, and the Baby can be more unpredictable and dangerous than the Old Man. I think of the ice and the village homes without any heating except for the kangri.

Like all children I ask the same question repeatedly, choosing exactly when I will incorporate the answer into my mind.

"It was very cold, but I was much younger. I wore my wooden sandals over the snow and the mud, kept a firepot ready and put my clothes over it so they were very warm when I wore them. I bathed quickly, shivering and sucking in little mouthfuls of air, and just as quickly put my clothes on. The worst was only a couple of times in winter, I had to bathe at the well just once a month, you see."

This story makes me cold, because I know that like all Kashmiri Brahmin women, she does not wear any trousers under her long dress, or any underwear, for that matter. I wonder about the freezing wind blowing about her legs, and yes, her buttocks, and other private parts. Why they dispensed with lingerie is still a mystery to me, and I have been offered various explanations.

We were often told that if the women's clothes touched their private parts they could not enter the prayer room or the kitchen without a bath, but mostly we did not know the reason why pandit women dispensed with underwear. This is how the dress code for women was and had always been. Men, like lamb and fish, are exempt from these strictures. The Muslim women, on the other hand, wear sensible and beautiful trousers under their shorter, knee-length dresses. I ask these questions now, but then, this is how it was.

The idea of naked legs in subzero temperatures is mind-boggling to me. Winter permanently colors and shapes us in Kashmir. There is no central heating anywhere in the city except in the main hospital. The government offices move, as they always have, to the winter capital, Jammu, where the season is snowless and milder. This annual flight has less to do with ensuring efficacy than with the fact that our royal family is from Jammu and does not like our winter. We who stay back in the valley love it and make ourselves comfortable. In my paternal grandfather Shyamji's house we have wood-burning stoves in a couple of rooms. My primary residence is at my father's father's house, which is just down the street from my mother's mother's house.

The snow and the cold last for almost half the year. Our winters have always been formidable, but so far we have taken hardly any technological steps to mitigate our experience of it. When I take a bath, two generations after my grandmother, the only improvement on her bathing odyssey is that for me the bathing water is hot. The bathroom in Shyamji's house, as it is everywhere in Kashmir, is cold except for the steam from the boiling hot water sloshing about in galvanized steel buckets. We do not have showers.

This is why the bathing room in traditional homes is always attached to the kitchen. This way it can share its fires. So it used to be in my house. The kitchen and the bathroom held a secret between them, their common wall split to create an enclosure big enough to hold an earthenware water tank. As the logs of wood in the kitchen were lit and the food was being cooked, the fire rose up in the hearth and spread to the base of the earthenware tank in the adjoining bathroom. The versatile fire cooked our food and heated up our bathwater simultaneously. Even after the kitchen was closed for the next meal the insulated enclosure kept the bathwater hot for almost the whole day.

Sadly, we succumbed to change and added a modern bathroom to the house. Like everything new, it is an extraneous structure. Now hot water has to be carried to our new bathroom after being heated in several large kettles of water on cooking hearths, or by electrical immersion rods. The water is boiled longer to keep it hot longer. The new bathroom is supposed to improve things, but in my opinion it is too cold, and all in all a pain.

When I bathe, Tulli, my paternal grandmother, warms my clothes by the wood-burning stove in the family room. When I am about done bathing I shout from the bathroom. Someone hurriedly brings my warmed clothes and hands them to me through a half-opened door, behind which I hide naked and shivering. My teeth are chattering, the mirror has steamed up, and my back aches from the cold. I frantically pull on the clothes, warming to life as they cover me, miraculously escaping death by freezing every time.

After I get dressed I run to the warm room and put on socks that I have knitted or my grandmother has knitted. I am glad to be free of the violent cold in the outside bathroom. My frozen jaw and shoulder muscles have contracted painfully, and they begin to thaw. It is an ordeal and a testament to the desire of us human beings to keep clean, even if our lives are lost in the process.

Unlike the bathing room, which is deep in the heart of traditional homes, the lavatory is separate and far from the main building. It is equipped with commodes that are removed and cleaned by a "sweeper" who belongs to a low caste even among the caste-less Muslims. Traditional folks squat in the lavatory; they do not sit on anything but their haunches, as they do not want any part of their body to touch the unclean outhouse. We have no choice but to make the freezing trudge to the outdoor lavatory several times a day. Then a revolution sweeps the lavatory, just as it did the bathing room, and we install modern toilets. Everyone is grateful for the "flush" system; aesthetically it is a great jump forward for all, particularly the "sweeper." Now he does not manually handle buckets of feces. He is required only to clean the bathroom cosmetically and make it shine.

A modern bathroom and hot water are fine; even so, having a bath every day in the cold season is something we dare not think about; it is like tempting fate. Even in my time we Kashmiris are not famous for bathing, and bathing with cold water is unheard of except by ascetics or when a price is being paid for deeds from this or another life.

✳ ✳ ✳

Dhanna's mind must have been on something else as she encountered the first icy splash on her back, as it froze her spine and set her teeth on edge. How did she manage after a wintry bath, walking back through the snow in her high wooden sandals to her mother's house without socks and underwear? She must have held her firepot strategically, giving herself some central heating as she made it back to the house at midnight.

I see her. Her head is covered with a shawl folded over eight-fold in a triangular shape, and so is most of her face. She scrambles into her bed as soon as she is indoors, and pulls the almost hard and heavy quilt around her. On top of the white quilt is a brown woolen blanket with a green stripe, an accent simultaneously decorative and austere. The blanket is woven to be twelve feet long and has to be folded once. Thus doubled it is the same length as the quilt. She makes a tent of the quilt with her knees, her firepot under her legs now, her toes still a little cold. Her mother serves her a hot meal in bed; she is almost entirely covered by the heavy bedding, only her head and right hand are available. After dinner she pulls the quilt over her head. Soon the steaming food spreads to her ears and toes and she is asleep, dreaming of things past and things to be. Like everyone else she goes to sleep with the firepot in the bed and through the night the coals burn to a fine hot ash that will start the fires of tomorrow.

Sometimes firepots overturn and beds and houses burn down. Almost everything is made of wood, but it is always agreed that the fire is the person's fault.

"You should know how to hold the kangri, everyone does it," we are told.

I hear this all the time.

It is too ancient and vital a system to come under any criticism. The firepot is like a limb to a person. Someone else has to take the blame. People say with pride that we Kashmiris are listed in the British medical textbooks. We are the only people in the world who suffer from "kangri cancer." People hold the kangri between their legs all the time, some even through summer, and this sometimes sets their inner thighs to rot.

I know that most of the older women have purple markings on their inner thighs where the kangri has cooked their blood vessels. I cannot say about the men, because at this point I am not even aware that men have inner thighs. But among the women adulthood and blue inner thighs seem to be synonymous, a sign of many years of hot fire held close to your heart and thighs, and the older the women, the deeper the purple.

The British medical texts do not really matter to me. I am more concerned about acquiring all the hallmarks of a seasoned woman. So, I endeavor to sit on the carpet as long as I can with a kangri full of flaming hot coals under my bent knees. This is how we all sit if we are to be modest. Even though clothed appropriately, we do not display our stomach and genital areas to open view by sitting in the lotus position. We sit that way only when praying or eating, when we are in receiving mode. Anyway, after a couple of weeks of kangri roasting I begin to see faint outlines of my inner thigh blood vessels, and run to show Tulli. She scolds me and says firmly that I am not to burn my legs with a kangri again.

I give up my quest readily. I have other distractions in winter. In Shyamji's house, where I live, we use wood-burning stoves rather than kangris. I think that the absence of a wood-burning stove in Dhanna's house had more to do with their ascetic lifestyle than finances. They certainly could have afforded all the wood-burning stoves they wanted. I go back to entertaining myself at home by roasting potatoes in the hot ash inside the woodstove, or grilling lamb liver or kidneys slapped onto the burning stove sides. Searing the raw meat on the hot iron fills the room with an appetizing aroma and fumes. On the stove top a kettle of water is always almost at the boil, at the ready for Western-style tea in a pot or for hand-and-face ablutions in the washbasin because we do not have running hot water.

The hot stove is the scene of all my culinary adventures. In addition to using its sizzling sides as a grill I use the stove top to heat milk with sugar and almonds in little aluminum containers which I then put out in the snow and ice overnight to make ice-milk. It's a treat I will enjoy in the warmth of our family room the next day. I offer it to the adults, but the ice is too hard and their teeth cannot take the frozen temperature. Hot and cold are good in a balance, but only in a balance. Having too much of one or the other is asking for trouble, and you better learn those lessons while you are still a child.

Heavy mattresses hang over the door to keep the three generations of chills out. Outside the icy street air is suffused with smoke from wood-burning stoves, cooking fires, and the sizzle of barbecued meat and fish in street shops. Freshly baked bread, hot to the touch, and vapors of steaming kettles of tea prepared by roadside vendors tantalize cold office-goers walking home from work. The lucky ones travel by tanga and the hard winter roads resound with the clip-clop of the hooves of caparisoned horses, slipping and sliding as they negotiate ice, exhaling clouds from their nostrils and teeth. Tanga-wallahs, bundled up in thick shawl blankets, crack their whip threateningly to prod the horses on. Every now and then the drivers' lips emerge from the warmth of their blankets to shout "Hosh!" to alert the pedestrians milling in the street. The few who possess cars are also bundled up because it is the fifties and there is no heating in the cars. These sights, smells, and sounds are all part of our winter existence and we revel in it. Snow-capped peaks and mountains run around us like a carousel and in winter the mountain passes are perilous. You travel into Kashmir in the winter only if you must.

Even at the best of times I am terrified of ever being cold and numb. My grandmother's penance for my mother and her siblings preoccupies me. I always ask her about it.

"Do you know that only those who accumulate the highest karma in their previous life are destined to see children play and hear their laughter in this life? I must have left something incomplete," says my grandmother, "and had to make up for it by doing penance in this life before I was given children. When you have to do something, you do it."

I look up at her, my mouth full of the green almonds she has given me, and I just nod to signify I understand. She gives me green walnuts as well, but always makes sure that while enjoying her treats I register what is real and important, so that I grow well inside and out.

Today she sits with her turbaned friend Kashi Nath on the wooden settee in the kitchen hall. Still looking at me she passes her hookah pipe to her husband's diminutive office clerk.

He takes it, head lowered, and puffs at it very softly, very deferentially. My grandmother and the clerk are partners in hookah-smoking, a sport her husband is aware of but not party to. They would not dream of puffing at the hookah in front of her husband, individually or together, but the kitchen is her arena. When my grandfather approaches her domain he comes in slow, deliberate, resounding steps so that she can put away what she does not want him to see. My grandmother and the frail clerk are companions, and the clerk listens to her as she talks. He rarely burdens her with his problems, although she is always solicitous. He is clean-shaven, but vast compensatory amounts of hair emanate from his ears.

Kashi Nath is the one who buys the tobacco on his way over to the house as he carries my grandfather's files from the office. For me he brings fine calico letter paper and pencils. My grandmother and he seem to enjoy a sweet-scented tobacco, which leaves treacly stains on the newspaper in which it is wrapped. From the looks and the smell and its molasses-like color I think it must taste sweet if eaten. I ask my grandmother, and she widens her eyes and sticks her tongue between her upper and lower teeth and shakes her finger. This mime leaves no uncertainty in my mind that what I have just said is something unmentionable. Girls my age cannot even think such thoughts.

Carefully Kashi Nath makes a little morsel of the sticky tobacco, places it in the terra-cotta chillum pipe, which he then places above the hookah, making a continuous tunnel from the chillum neck, through the hookah and the water in its belly, through the hookah pipe to his mouth. Then he picks up the small tongs hanging from the side of the chillum, and selects a few hot chinar coals from his kangri and places them on the tobacco in the chillum. A few puffs later the coals light up in the tiny clay brazier. A few more puffs and gurgles in the hookah stomach, and the smoke cycle is complete and working and their ritual has commenced.

There is something very calm about the whole event; the sweet smelling smoke they puff out in discreet mouthfuls heightens this sense.

I busy myself with the clean outer layer of newspaper from the tobacco package. The scrap is full of dark black print but completely illegible to me. It is written in Persian script, but it follows Western protocol, with headlines over columns in bold large letters, and news in small print, six columns to a page. I try to make sense of it, but even the numerals are in Arabic.

My grandmother turns to her smoking buddy and says, "She reads everything, even tobacco paper."

Sitting in a respectful posture, Kashi Nath looks up and shakes his head from side to side in a mixture of approval and concern for a girl who will not even leave a piece of stained tobacco paper alone. Everyone reads all the newspapers they can, both in English and Urdu, but it is primarily a male pastime.

We do not have our own script, even though we have a great literary tradition that has been followed in borrowed scripts. Now we all use English and Urdu and Hindi when we write. Intimate conversations are held in Kashmiri, formal ones in Urdu, and when someone wants to shut down the opposition in an authoritative way, a couple of sentences in English usually does the trick. The English are gone but not forgotten.

There is something comfortable and secure about our unlikely threesome. I pick up my pencil and sketch the two of them, Dhanna and her friend, puffing away at the hookah. They see the drawing and it sends my grandmother into paroxysms of laughter. The clerk wants to laugh out loud but knows better, and all you can see is his shoulders shaking softly as he smiles.

"Mad little girl," she says. "Now don't show that to anyone."

She pulls my dress over my knees; she is always doing that. If she had her way I would be wearing a *shalwar kameez* instead of a frock, which would cover everything from below the neck down to my toes. But my father's family is foolishly modern and she stays in her place. After all, her daughter is someone else's property now.

Relatives come and go to Dhanna's house. They bring her really crisp lotus root, or batter-fried lotus root, pink and white lotus flowers, or lotus seeds raw, or ripening, or ripe with hard black shells. Or they bring blueberries, mulberries, or fried or roasted peas, or kohlrabi, or pickles, or spices. We are too cold a place to grow sugarcane so we hardly have any indigenous sweetmeats except rice pudding. Dhanna's visitors take back an equally eclectic assortment of edibles gifted by her. They are intimidated by her, but love her; her seniority is a powerful thing, but I think her honesty has something to do with it as well. No one except me even gives the hookah a second look; it is taken for granted and is nothing out of the ordinary as far as they are concerned.

I wonder what the Irish nuns at my school will say if I tell them that my grandmother smokes a hubble bubble with a thin short man in a ponderous saffron turban. I, who have just played St. Bernadette of Lourdes for the Bishops from south India! But the nuns have the Irish Fathers from the boys' school visit them and join them for dinner and sing songs. Besides they teach us songs like "What shall we do with the drunken sailor ear-lie in the morning," so I suspect they will not be too horrified. Still, the saffron turban and the bushy whiskers might be too much for them.

✻✻✻

When did my grandmother start smoking?

I cannot talk about her hookah in my other grandfather's house. Once when I announced her smoking activities at dinnertime everyone was quiet. They know, but they do not talk about it because it is not what sophisticated modern women do. I am told in hushed tones that we do not talk about these things. Shyamji has a mischievous twinkle in his eye; he is very fond of my maternal grandparents but also loves it when children come out with embarrassing truths.

We have a hookah in my house, too, but only Shyamji smokes it. His hookah has a lot more metal than wood, is aquiline and tall, and the pipe is much longer so that my grandfather can puff at it while sitting on the sofa or chair as well. He shares his hookah with the odd guest. Once a year he also shares his hookah with his head farmer who brings us the rice every year from our ancestral fields.

The farmers from our village arrive unannounced one day at the end of the harvesting season, followed by a long line of donkeys carrying grain in burlap sacks hanging one on each side. The exact day is a surprise in a phone-less world, but we seem to have a sense of their impending arrival. The farmers bring in the sacks on their shoulders and take them to the kitchen area where the granary is. The beasts temporarily populate our street, incongruous visitors in a neighborhood of suburban houses.

Only the head farmer comes into our informal sitting room, carefully leaving his richly woven straw sandals outside on the coir doormat. He is tall and gaunt, tanned by the sun to a deep brown, and has extraordinarily long feet, typical of villagers, according to common belief. Bits of mud are caked on his toes, but he is wearing his best caftan and a formal brown wool shawl-blanket is folded on his shoulder. On his psoriasis-ravaged head he wears a pointed white skullcap embroidered with gold thread. The head farmer sits right next to my grandfather, shares his bolster cushion as he sits down on the carpet; even sitting down he is a good head taller than my grandfather. The farmer is quiet and dignified and my grandfather makes perfunctory inquiries about the rice fields; too much respect for the farmer precludes asking for details.

Our Muslim servants will make the farmers salt tea with milk and give them bagels from a Muslim baker. The farmers might eat fruit or nuts or sugar candy at our house, but they will not eat anything cooked on the heathen fires in our kitchen. My grandfather is wearing a pheran but his shawl-blanket is pashmina and he wraps it over his left shoulder like a toga. He looked like Julius Caesar, I always thought; there was a definite likeness in his profile and hairline. Shyamji will change after lunch into a tweed suit and go to teach at his college or go out for a walk, while the farmer is true to his caftan and knee-length trousers. Sometimes my mother tells me I have the feet of a farmer because I take the biggest size in women's shoes.

When the farmers leave after being rested and fed, and our granary is replenished, a general sense of security prevails. The rice grains are stored in man-high earthen vessels in our storehouse, which is built near the kitchen but separate from the house. The vessels are shaped like Morgiana's pots from the story of Ali Baba, and can easily hide a person. We say in Kashmir that if you have rice and greens, you have everything you need, and the fact is, for generations that is all we had.

The donkeys are also relieved, for a couple of reasons. For one thing, the bulging sacks of grain are off their backs, and our street is littered with the evidence from the other.

The food grains assure us at a depth not easily plumbed and

for this as for everything else there is a reason. We know that time comes full circle and what has gone before we will face again. Legend has it that after the last cataclysmic deluge in our valley, a bird from paradise dropped a grain of barley into the waters, which receded, and Kashmir arose again.

The primordial flood receded but the flood line has remained forever inside us, and our waters and their contents permeate our inner and outer lives. So we are circumspect and try not to provoke the forces of nature that have ruled our destinies so impetuously in the past and will almost certainly do so in the future. We do not take the farmers' arrival every year for granted. As long as we are warm in the winter and we have food to eat, we are grateful to be alive in a beautiful valley.

Unlike Morgiana we have nothing to hide. Our tall jars are full of rice, lentils, beans, and rich yellow mustard seed oil. Our dark yielding soil will easily provide the greens we crave in all their varieties, wild and tame, and our waters will give us sweet mirror carp, native river salmon and brook trout. Our backyard outside the kitchen has a high pile of stacked dry timber, neatly chopped into the right size for our kitchen and stove fires, even though winter is a couple of months away. Our family is well and we are God-fearing. What more can we want?

At night my grandparents, the householders, go to bed satisfied and happy that at least for the year ahead, until the farmers come back again, we have all we need.

Mothers

There are mothers and there are mothers. Every mother's story is different, but the roots and the aims are the same for all. In Kashmir, when we help our mothers with anything, they tell us, "A mother without a daughter is like a boat without oars."

Even when Dhanna's children are grown up with grown-up children she remembers each time she gave birth as if it were yesterday.

After my mother was born—in fact, after each subsequent delivery—there is a month of bed rest for Dhanna. She can only eat foods with the right natures, and she is rigorously massaged from top to toe. On the last day of confinement after birth, be it summer or winter, she is given a hot bath to expel any toxins not yet banished by the peppery meatballs, massage, and herbal teas she has been given. The bathwater is as hot as it is possible for a woman to bear and the room is misty with the vapors of birthing herbs. The doors and windows are shut tight, and will remain so until she is done bathing. Then she is put into warm clothes, helped back into bed, fed yet another flaming spicy meal, and tucked in for the night. This ritual will see her safely out of one delivery and prepare for the next, and her feeling of being well cared for will last her a lifetime.

This is a changeable time; there is new life in the house and all under the roof are vulnerable. Everyone cups his or her hands around the lamp and the flame it bears. If someone knocks at the door it is opened slowly and never with the baby in arms, because the child still smiles at the angels it has had to leave to come down to earth. The mother is not exposed to strangers, or cold, or foods that are intrinsically cold no matter how hot you may serve them, nor can she be jeopardized by harsh winds. Any chill, or fright, or sadness at this time when the mother's bones have softened to make way for the child may make a permanent imprint. All the women know what to do, they have all been through this season, and they participate in it wholeheartedly; they understand this sacred time, and their knowledge is as old and as valuable as the ritual. The first surviving child of Dhanna and Babuji is my mother, and she is named Katyayani, after the Tiger Lady.

After the month is over, it is back to normal for everyone, except for the special care that has to be taken in nursing the baby. My aunt arrives soon after my mother, and a wet nurse is found among the married women with slightly older children because Dhanna is too weak to nurse two at the same time. The youngest is nursed the longest before he is also weaned by rubbing bitter herbs on her nipples. He loses all desire for his mother's breasts.

My grandparents love their three children as prized possessions and watch incredulously as they fill up their days. The children play outside until it is dark and have to be called many times before they come in for dinner. They are so tired from play that they fall asleep as they are being fed, but are nudged repeatedly to take another bite. Somehow they make it down to the last morsel, the most important morsel, for he who has the last morsel of his food will become a monarch. This inducement works even with sleepy and dog-tired children. After everyone has been put to bed my grandfather tiptoes around his sleeping children to make sure they are well covered by quilts and blankets.

My mother's friends, children of her father's friend, live two houses down the street. My father is one of the children. One day in the spring when Katyayani is about twelve years old she is forbidden from going to my father's house. Shortly thereafter my parents are engaged. On the engagement day my paternal aunts and uncles, all under twelve, bring my mother sweet clotted cream with pistachios in a silver bowl from which my father has been fed a spoonful already. Shyly, Katyayani takes a tiny spoonful of the cream, fed by her best friend and now her sister-in-law to be. Then she wears the clothes and the jewelry they have brought her, and everyone sits down to an elaborate meal. My father is at home with his parents. Now he will come to his fiancée's house only on his marriage day, when all his relatives will accompany him in a long procession and he will take my mother home as his bride.

After the engagement Katyayani's friends come over to play with her, but she still is not allowed to go to my father's house. This is fine until summer starts and the usual picnics follow. Now Katyayani is kept at home and her mother stays behind with her. The twelve-year-old cares more for her friends and the boat rides than the upcoming marriage and cries and wants to go on the picnic, but the wedding date has been fixed and the question does not arise. She climbs up to the attic that is on the fourth floor in their house. From here she can see the street and the fur caps of the tanga drivers, and the manes of the horses, the baskets of food, the heads of her friends and siblings and the other people from the two families, all setting off in the direction of the Mughal Gardens. She refuses to eat anything all day, but her mother manages to persuade her by dinnertime. I know this because Mother tells me this many times, even when she is a grandmother.

When my mother was married two years later, she basically went from one lap to the next, just around the corner. Whenever she felt homesick she just asked a sister-in-law to accompany her and they both walked over to my grandmother's house where they would be fussed over and pampered and given tea and sweet flaky butter biscuits with poppy seeds kept for just such occasions. Katyayani was given a trousseau of gold, silver, pashmina, cooking utensils, saris, chosen with all the care lavished on a first child's wedding. Since my aunt was up next, and quite soon, most things were bought in doubles. The saddle and reins were ready for my aunt, they said, and now it was just a matter of looking for a horse.

My mother is fourteen and my father is nineteen. He goes off to engineering college and she stays with his family, going to her parents' house as usual, only now she stays for extended visits.

One by one all of Dhanna's children are married. All that remains to be done now is wait for the grandchildren. When my mother and aunts have children exactly the same procedures are followed as when they were born. The children are delivered at home, now a female doctor is present instead of a midwife, but everything else is the same. The children are born here in the valley and everyone knows what to do. Mothers and children are safely nurtured through their vulnerable time. Katyayani becomes a mother under the tutelage of her mother, this is how it has always been and they are certain that this is how it will always be. They cannot even imagine otherwise.

The children are young, the parents are young, and the grandparents are young, and there is always a great grandparent or two somewhere in the house. There is a lot of coming and going, family life occupies our days fully and we love it.

Then, out of the blue, as they often do, sorrow and worry made an appearance in Dhanna's house and refused to go away despite our prayers and offerings. My maternal grandfather fell ill. He did not smoke or drink but developed cirrhosis of the liver, which remained undiagnosed for too long because it is such an improbable disease for such an upright man. He was mistakenly treated for a kidney ailment and naturally his condi-

tion worsened by the day. We tried everything, the best medicines, even going to a mad Muslim hermit for answers. We
weighed Babuji against rice grains and distributed the grains to
the poor. We took him up to the mountains for a long stay and
to a healing spring, but it was too late and nothing worked.

When my grandfather died I went to live with Dhanna for a
short time. As I remember it, I thought then that he was a very
old man, but he was not quite sixty at the time of his death, and
his wife was even younger than that.

❀❀❀

Dhanna is alone now. During the day she sits with other women
in ritual mourning, accepting condolences offered only by silent grief and glances. She has removed the hundred-year-old
red and gold brocade cuffs accenting her dress sleeves, she can
wear only plain white cuffs on her sleeves now. Nothing is said,
people come into the house, take off their shoes outside the sitting room and quietly find a place on the carpet, the men in one
room and the women in another.

A large male figure stands at the door with his hands on the
door frame and, without entering the women's room, says to her,
"Sister, take heart. Your husband was like a brother to me. I have
fixed a pension on you to honor your incorruptible husband."

Then the Prime Minister of Kashmir leaves, in a flurry of
officials and assistants. He is the head of the government now,
but he was born the son of a midwife. Like most of his colleagues
he is a Muslim, but this thought does not occur to anyone then.
It is interesting only in hindsight.

Soon people stop coming to my grandmother's house and
all the rituals are done, but she continues to mourn. That is
when I go to stay with her in her large empty house. I sleep in
her room now; my bed is made on the carpet. She sleeps on the
large bed she shared with my grandfather, with its heavy posters

and rounded legs, the dark walnut wood shining under white cotton sheets. She tosses in bed, and sometimes kicks back the covers, stretching her legs, and wails out to her dead husband at night, calling him by a name she has not used openly before. That is when I know the difference between a husband and a lover, and she has lost both in one strike.

She is an old woman within a week and continues to age rapidly. Her ankles are so thin they look swordlike; she has tied protective talisman anklets made of black threads on them. My grandmothers are co-mothers to me, and their lives, their joys and losses affect me as if they were my own mother. I wonder, "What is she thinking of now?"

Always fastidious, Dhanna walks gingerly on her high wooden Kashmiri clogs with the decorative red-and-green carved pattern. The platform is a good four inches above the summer ground, but she is determined to keep clear of the snow should it arrive. You never know. Once it snowed in April, just as it was turning into May. We don't easily forget twists and turns like that.

It looks as though she spends all her time looking for something. She breaks off branches of the poplar trees in her backyard and plants them in the generous soil, soon creating a small poplar forest. She keeps up her vegetable garden and sends me out in the early afternoon to bring in baby eggplants and crunchy green chilies, which she cooks with potatoes, and we eat this with fragrant rice and yogurt. Sometimes she makes batter-fried pumpkin flowers for me, and when I persuade her to have some she agrees quite readily. I have a feeling she liked that snack as a child and that is why she made it. I don't recall ever having requested it. Meat and fish are rarely on the menu now, but our meals are always delicious. Together we eat in silence.

After the death of my grandfather my grandmother resigned herself to everything and uncharacteristically let things slip by her. I did not see her laugh for many months, through fall, winter, and spring. When summer came around once again and started in earnest I decided that it was my turn to make Grandma laugh.

I joke about little things and try to cook for her, but it is a mess always and she cannot but be amused. Dhanna loves her vegetable garden and her poplar trees, so we spend a lot of time in the backyard. She makes little mud dams to channel water into the right vegetable beds, and when we walk on their narrow banks, we slip now and then into the just-irrigated muddy patch. Then we go to the garden hose and wash our feet clean; we are both wearing clogs now, mandatory footwear for the vegetable garden. When autumn comes we pluck and eat only the ripe fruit from her trees. Grandma is terrified that I may eat an unripe fruit and die from it. The pear tree beckons mischievously with its entanglement of twisted branches. Some of the pears are sweet and some are not.

I know, because I am perpetually trying them out, secretly, over my grandmother's predictions that I will have diarrhea, dysentery, and other stomach ailments that routinely used to fell children when she was young. Now we have potassium permanganate, penicillin, and other antibiotics, but she believes more in fate. In the end I believe my grandmother's concern for me, the child of her absent daughter, brought her back to worrying, laughing, feeling.

Gradually the smile returns to her face. We are both comedians for each other's sake now. At night she takes out her perfect teeth, and we both collapse with laughter at how very old she looks toothless. She loves to laugh at herself. That was the other thing they said about her. They said that she laughed until she lost her voice and the tears ran down her face.

I help Dhanna with her bath in the bathing room behind her kitchen wall. In my hand I hold the yogurt–mustard seed oil mixture she uses as a conditioner and nutrient between the two cake soap shampoos and rinses she gives her hair with every bath. Then I pass her the square wooden comb with the million teeth and inlaid mirrors that she keeps on the shelf. She parts her hair in the middle and carefully combs out the length of it. I pour her bathwater in large jugfuls over her hair and her back for a final rinse as she sits squatting like a Degas woman on the low wooden bath seat. When she is done, I hand her warmed clothes and her kangri on which they were warmed and she goes into the sitting room. Sometimes after Dhanna bathes I make her some green tea leaves boiled in milk with slivered blanched almonds, sugar, and cardamom, a favorite of mine even today. We sip the hot milk–tea sitting across from each other, she from the brass khos which she holds in a towel, and I from a china cup so that I don't scald my inept lips.

Together we make the slow move out of sorrow and into life. Having seen my grandmother somewhat restored I return to my paternal grandfather's house.

๛๛๛

Everything changes and only what is real is constant.

When my maternal grandfather Babuji fell ill, changes started to be made in his house, one after the other, almost imperceptibly. His horse-drawn carriage had given way to a more comfortable but small British-made car. The carriage house became a garage. Then the car was gone because my grandfather was too ill to go to his office or to his village at harvesttime. The farmers brought the harvest to the house and the garage became a storehouse for the grains from our rice fields.

The quantity of rice grains was large enough, but it was the varieties of rice from Babuji's fields that were the real envy of the neighborhood. All the grains were native to the soil, and since we had not heard of hybridization yet, or chemical fertilizer or pesticides, every good harvest was a blessing. Our ancestral fields grew pearl-like rice, and sweet red rice, which is only served with fish, and rice that naturally carries such a subtle blend of flavors that it is called *mushk-i-budhijh,* the Kashmiri equivalent of bouquet garni. For fear of the evil eye, my grandmother sent the grains in discreet installments by the sackful to the recently mechanized hulling machine. Then the rice was stored for the year.

The year I was born this annual ritual was brought to an abrupt halt. Everything stood still when the Afghan frontiersmen penetrated the valley. Even though we returned home safe, and the scourge was removed, we were still shaken and no one wanted to leave the safety of his or her home. That autumn we hulled the rice ourselves, pounding the grain in the backyard in our giant granite mortar and five-foot tall wood pestle made from an entire tree trunk.

"Fortunately the tribesmen were easily recognized," says Dhanna.

The sudden and brutal intrusion into our placid lives is not laid to rest until decades later, and we talk about it often; it seems to come up in the middle of many conversations as a marker of time and change. We talk about how in 1947 the Indian army was called in to repel the Afghans, but young men from the valley had also gathered to form an irregular volunteer corps to defend the valley. My uncle and his friends from the neighborhood went to fight in the mountain forests.

"When the fighting ceased the entire neighborhood waited on the main road looking for their boys among the bedraggled, exhausted young men returning in trucks. Some of the mothers had to return home empty-handed and bereft," says Shyamji.

My father's family was overjoyed to see their son return, but the neighborhood mourned in perpetuity the loss of his brave young friend from the house next door.

We rush to embrace my uncle initially, but wiser counsel prevails and we have to hold back until the old family barber is summoned and my uncle is shaved and shorn. Then he sheds all his clothing on the lawn, right there among the hydrangea and the roses, and is given a good dousing with disinfectant, scrubbed with soap, and bathed with scalding water. Uncle dries himself, laughing at the spectacle he has become for his neighbors and family. Then he is handed his clothes and brought into the house with embraces and kisses. His discarded clothing, alive with lice, is set afire in the granite walkway leading to our porch. As a child growing up he was always getting into trouble; he caused his parents a great amount of grief because he was so irrepressible. But it seems he has finally come a long way from the child who steals women's clothes as they bathe by the riverside. No longer does his mother have to evade questions about him.

No one has to bathe in the river anymore, even though we are told that river water is more effective in immunizing one against childhood disease than all the vaccinations and inoculations that we suburban people are prone to. Now we bathe in the river only when we go up to the mountains in the summer where no one can see us. We also bathe at sacred springs when we visit our shrines and holy places. The water is crystal clear and delicious, not too many immunizing bacteria here, but plenty of spiritual protection.

My uncle's temporary bout with army life was followed by a lifetime's distance from all things military, but he was always an activist. While in college he became quite radical, diligently contributing to Soviet magazines and literature from Red China, but when the pendulum had settled in the middle, as it must, he became a bureaucrat of the most dedicated kind. On the other hand my quiet father became an engineer, then gave up the predictable life to become an army officer, eventually going to battle like his brother, two decades later in the east of India, in the Bangladesh war.

My father's army career meant that every couple of years or so he would be posted to a new place. So my mother and sister and brother joined him after some time. I stayed behind with my grandparents for many reasons, the chief one being that my grandfather could not bear to let me go. I think they also felt that three children would be too much for my mother to handle. I was satisfied with the arrangement, happy to have everyone's attention to myself. In any event, we had only a vague idea that in our extended family life we had our own nuclear family. It was not something that was given much prominence; the larger tribe was crucial. Even when my mother and father were present, my grandparents were the de facto parents and heads of the household. Besides, I was already in school, and who better to guide a promising student like me than my grandfather, one of the most revered professors in Kashmir?

My parents came to Kashmir every summer for long holidays and we spent the winter holidays with them. After my parents and siblings went back I went about my business as usual, going over to my maternal grandmother's house almost every day. Sometimes I went to see her several times a day, it was so close. Back at home I sat with my grandfather on our porch, sharing the delights and the dramas that we encountered every day. I was a full-fledged member of the household, and far from feeling that I was not in my own home, luxuriated in being the only grandchild present. I have never felt so at home anywhere else.

When the time came for me to graduate from childhood to adolescence and marriageability, my mother's presence in my life returned to the same extent that it had been when I was an infant. Marriage was an undertaking that required more energy, money, and time than was possible for grandparents to provide. These transitions were so old and well known that the changes were made without disruption and everyone knew what was expected of them.

As I become a teenager, so does Kashmir in its democratic incarnation. Like me, our surroundings are changing. The farmers declare that the land they till and its produce belongs to them, the politicians concur, and so begrudgingly do the landowners. We now get a fraction of the harvest and have to supplement our rice grains with government-issued rations. Soon there is nothing in Dhanna's garage but a few sacks of grain, some household junk, and a carriage wheel. The few donkeys who come from the rice fields bring grain that occupy only a corner of the storehouse. The family talks about the time when the rice arrived from the village and there was so much of it that the storehouse was ready to burst with the grains.

But prosperity has spread from a few to many across the valley, there are many more people, there is a greater need for our natural resources. Trees are becoming increasingly scarce from legal and illegal logging, and smoke from log fires, once a sign of comfort, is not seen as desirable anymore. Like the bathing room and the lavatory, the old kitchen with its heartwarming fires and ample chimney is also retired, and now we have cooking gas and electricity. A shiny new gas cooking range is put into the kitchen, complete with a new steel table. The cooking hearth sullenly turns dark and quiet. I hate the steel and the practicality and the newness of the kitchen and I am grateful that in spite of purchasing electric room heaters we still use the wood-burning stoves in our living quarters. By the time I am ready to go to college so many old ways have been thrown completely overboard. We seem to have lost some of our complacency and contentment, although this is nothing compared to what we are about to see down the road. It is just as well that we cannot even dream of what lies in the future for us.

We might have a modern kitchen now, but I look forward to the formal occasions when our old cook, Sudarshan, now a venerable grandfather, comes back to cook for us. He will never touch a gas range if his life depends on it, and within moments of his arrival the old hearth fires are ablaze once again, crackling as they joyously send fountains of red and yellow embers into the chimney. The flames remember and find their way to the base of an entombed man-tall vessel, heating up the water inside. We now use the hot water from the old bathroom only for doing the dishes in the kitchen, but it feels good to have the medieval water heater called up from retirement once in a while.

Our cook has come to our house to prepare one of the summer banquets given by my grandfather. Any excuse is good enough for Shyamji. We are happy to wait and suffer the torture of enduring a day filled with appetizing whiffs and vapors just for the glory of the meal at night. The more time something takes, the better it always is.

He looks right at place, that old chef, with his crown of red hair and walrus mustache, as he busies himself restoring in a small measure a part of life as we knew it just some years ago. When we eat, we have to admit that the quality of the food from these ferocious fires is far superior to anything a modern appliance can produce.

Sudarshan says, "Real food can only be prepared on traditional equipment. How can I take red-hot coals out of the gas range?" In Kashmiri excellent, worthwhile, and real are the same word.

Perfectionist and traditionalist that he is, Sudarshan needs the coals for final touches to his dishes and, equally important, for his hookah. He cooks in earthenware pots with concave lids that he seals with dough putty. Then he puts red-hot coals on top of the concave lid, effectively creating an oven of sorts where his dishes acquire their last hours of heat seasoning and flavor. This is just one of his secrets. The daughters and daughters-in-law of our house flatter him and bring him tea and finally persuade him to let them write down some of his recipes. He can neither read nor write but his children are well educated, and that is his accomplishment as well, and he takes pride in it.

"It's gold," he says of his secret recipes, laughing between puffs at the hookah pipe that he holds in the side of his mouth, "A poor man's gold. Here, I give it to you. What will you remember?" He knows he is a genius, but like a true artist he loves appreciation. I remember everything, and remember it well. I will inherit all the recipes, and I know just how to prepare them. Decades later I will put all my recollected recipes into a book for my children, and say to myself, "What will they remember, when Kashmir is like Shangri-la, a matter of myth, an eternal vale, never to be seen again in this life?" To my delight my children can tell the difference between a real *roghanjosh* and a pseudo-concoction. When I replicate some of those family meals in my own home, I close my eyes, surround myself with the aromas, and pretend that I am in Kashmir.

I know exactly how Sudarshan's recipes have to be prepared because that crusty old man has decided quite arbitrarily very early in my childhood that I, the youngest child in the house, am to be his official taste tester. So, on big cooking occasions, on his instructions, I sit on the low wooden ledge separating the kitchen from the shoe-contaminated rest of the house. He, whom everyone fears, looks anxiously at my child's face for signs as I pronounce judgment. Of course, I never say anything about the ingredients because I do not know what he uses or should use, but he checks my pulse by asking if the salt is right. And I am usually on the mark, and although I think I am checking the salt, he relies on my facial expression to judge for himself. I don't know if he does this because he is superstitious, and thinks I bring him good luck. Perhaps he has intuitively guessed that I will grow up to love really good food.

The banquet culminates in the old man appearing with a tray of shoulder lamb chops cooked in milk, saffron, and herbs, then deep-fried in clarified butter and finally decorated with pure silver leaf that whispers as he moves the tray around. The trick is to get each piece of lamb to have two long ribs, a layer of lean meat, a layer of soft fat, and a paper-thin skin of tallow on top. Except for the bones every bit of the kabargah piece melts in your mouth. When the guests compliment him Sudarshan is quietly pleased.

We are careful when we talk to him because he has a short temper, and this is why he is also the family pickle maker. Every year at a certain season he comes to our house to fill cream-and-brown ceramic jars with vegetables pickled in crushed mustard seeds, spices, and mustard oil. It is a lengthy ceremony and we prepare for his arrival by sun-drying the vegetables for a couple of days. Then he mixes the vegetables and the pickling spices in a huge round brass tray. Finally, he smokes the jar with asafetida smoke and stuffs the vegetables and spices into the jars, pounding down the mixture with his hand to expel air.

It takes almost the whole day to accomplish a year's worth of pickles, and the exercise is punctuated with different breads and cups of sweet or salt green tea, and hookah puffs. He loves the salt tea that we Kashmiris drink. We add a tiny pinch of soda to the boiling tea, and when we add milk the tea immediately turns salmon pink. We do the master cook the added honor of topping off the tea with layers of clotted cream from the saucepans of cooling boiled milk that await dispensation in the kitchen. No one ever brings up the fact that he is asked to make the pickles because he is considered to be a hot-tempered man. His red hair is ample proof of this fact, according to us. These are self-evident truths, and we never doubt them.

When our old chef comes to cook for us the hierarchy in the kitchen changes. All our servants, Muslim and Hindu, consider him an Ustad, a master and the most senior, and pay him due respect. Like him most of the kitchen staff came to us when young, sometimes when they were mere children, sent by their families to supplement a village income. In time most of them became like family. My grandparents arranged marriages or better jobs for them and sent them off to set up their own homes. They return often for a visit or when they need help in some matter, or when we call them for help.

After Sudarshan leaves, the junior servants carry the cream-and-brown ceramic jars upstairs to a sunny spot in the attic. There the pickles ferment, and are ready to be eaten at the appropriate season. When ready the pickles should cut a red swath down a pile of fluffy boiled rice.

The pickles are definitely ready in time for the Winter Moonless Night when we serve the good spirits who surround the house their annual dinner. We cook a special meal of their favorite food and place it outdoors for them, preferably on the wooden steps leading up to the storehouse where the grains are stored. The *yakshas* have a taste for the mortal life and on their feast day expect *khechhri,* rice with mung beans and lamb. Their cuisine travels all the way to England where it is served as kedgeree at breakfast.

We have an indoor deity as well, our house spirit, and he has his own special day. There are many alleged sightings of the deity, mostly in the attic where he lives, usually only by adults seeking to keep children in tow and out of the attic where there are many works in progress. We partake of the meal cooked in the house god's honor after we place his share, topped by a raw fish, on a table in the attic landing.

The fact is that all these tasty offerings go to the neighborhood cats, we know that, but the question of voicing this reality does not arise. Like most Brahmin households we keep neither cats nor dogs in the house, so it is easy for us children to believe that unseen deities consume the offerings. The truth is that no one wants to upset the natural order of things. Even those of us with advanced science degrees dare not tamper with fate by suggesting that the spirits do not exist.

We diligently repeat our seasonal activities year after year, observing good and bad days. We know from tales handed down through the generations that our life in the valley has always been precarious, so we like to assure ourselves of continuity in spite of overwhelming historical odds. We welcome new members of the tribe and honor those passed; it is a thread that passes from generation to generation, like a lifeline from our ancients to our future. When my maternal grandfather passed away, Dhanna honored him by observing his death rituals every year, as did his children. The mountains remained unmoving, mesmerized by their reflection in the lakes, as they watched us mortals go about our business.

⚜⚜⚜

Our relatives are with us, those that are alive, and those that have left us. If we forget even those long gone they remind us of their power in discomfiting ways. We may manage to skip their wrath, but we can be certain that they will hold our children hostage. So, we take care of them. If we fall behind in any way they come to remind us. And that is when we experience earthquakes.

Whenever we have an earthquake, we have to run out immediately and splash a bucket of water on the verandah. Our ancestors are thirsty and have come to ask for water. One night there is a severe earthquake and everyone scrambles out of bed and into the garden. One of the women runs out entirely naked, like a silver streak in the moonlight, a joy to behold. Her mother-in-law covers her with a shawl. Scandalized living relatives are somewhat mollified, but our ancestors, no longer obligated to pretend, take their own sweet time to go home that night.

Mercifully, no one remembers a really destructive earthquake, and we thank ourselves for that. We are Shaivite Brahmins and believe it is because we chant mantras to Shiva, our favorite of the Trinity of Brahma, Vishnu, and Shiva.

Shiva and his consort live in the temple crowning the hill that stands in the heart of town. The Destroyer God depicted by a phallic stone lingam, is ensconced in a stone depiction of the female, and the balance created by the fusion of both energies keeps things quiet. We children have been told in hushed tones that the hill is actually a dormant volcano, although no one can remember the last eruption. The temple is built on the crater. Our valley carries within its tectonic plates the seeds of its own destruction, and we all know that these are always moving around in a subterranean snake kingdom. This movement can blow up in our face anytime, so we pray, the Hindus in our way and the Muslims in theirs, whenever there is an earthquake, and we grow up hearing these chants. All this makes good sense to us; we have many earthquakes, but the volcano remains dormant.

The Muslims have no use for Shiva but we pandits climb the hill and visit the temple as often as we can in the summer. Having made an arduous climb to the crater-top temple, we offer prayers and acquire virtue. But we are famished after the climb, so we rush down on the other side of the hill toward self-indulgence at a picnic on Dal Lake. We are emulating Shiva, combining asceticism and sensuality, perhaps this is why he appeals to us, we are always looking for a good time whenever we can find it. We take good care of our minor deities, but the wedding anniversary of Shiva, which falls in the winter, is the central part of the Kashmiri Hindu calendar.

The menu for this most important holiday is fixed and nothing can be deleted. We cannot give in to whimsical cravings; we only add items that can be repeated every year. Our menu is derived from our winter foods, which are exotic. We eat wild geese, which have flown all the way from Siberia, wild fowl with fluorescent turquoise and gold heads; we eat sun-dried tomatoes, gourds, and eggplants, sun-dried fruits, and dried fish. When we cook dried fish the house is filled with its overpowering odor, and although we joke about it and walk around with our fingers holding our noses, it is a winter dish we relish tremendously. Fresh vegetables and fruits are hard to come by in the winter and have to be captured at the right time in the summer. When the air is the driest and hottest we string up necklaces of fruits and vegetables and hang them to dry in our attic to preserve them for the winter.

✻✻✻

Shivratri celebrations go on for several days, just as do our own weddings. On the main day of "The Perfect Marriage," the one we aspire to, our priest officiates at our family prayers and only then can we partake of the feast prepared for the occasion. The priest starts at home in the old city and works his way through his congregation, finally arriving at our home very late at night. We are quite starved by the time he arrives, but we have to wait, sometimes until midnight. When the services are over we serve the married couple everything we are going to eat, but being deities they also get a whole raw fish, nature unimpaired by human enhancement. Only when this is done can we eat.

Shiva and his consort are everywhere in the valley, but the preeminent deity for us is Shakti, the female consort, the half that breathes life and energy into Shiva. Naturally the Goddess has many more shrines than the God. In a couple of the shrines the gift of choice for the Lady who rides a Tiger is a one-piece offering of the trachea, lungs, and liver of a goat or lamb. The Muslim butcher knows just how to prepare this offering, which we take up to the shrine where the raw meat is whirled into the sky. The flesh and blood whirligig soars into the heavens and it is received within moments, courtesy of circling kites adept at the ritual.

Some of the temples of the Goddess are strictly vegetarian, and to the most sacred of all of these we, growers of paddy, take rice pudding, which we call *khir,* the offering special to this deity. This shrine is a haven of peace. The clear blue-green spring surrounding the temple is in the middle of a garden of chinars. We pray that when we go to Khir Bhawani the spring waters will be clear. When the waters turn dark we are apprehensive because we know that some evil is about to descend upon our valley. The temple precincts are surrounded by Muslim homes and some of these homes have always been vegetarian.

At Shivratri we invite friends of other religious persuasions to our house for meals. We also send fruits and nuts to our older Muslim neighbors, while their children come over to our house for lunch or dinner. In turn we look forward to eating at their house on the two Eids celebrated by Muslims. For those members of my family who do not eat at a Muslim home, our hosts send a packet of uncooked lamb to our house. Our cooks will prepare the meat, and then it is fine for everyone to eat. Somehow it is the cooking that is a problem. Almost all our butchers are Muslim, and in a heartily nonvegetarian valley, they always prosper.

Our butcher, though hearty-looking, wears a meager beard that he has been encouraging to grow presumably since it first appeared many years ago. He has intellectual aspirations that he nurtures similarly and when he comes to collect his payments he sometimes discusses Sufi poetry with my grandfather. The butcher prefers to discourse with my grandfather in English, perhaps to give himself some much-needed practice.

On one Eid afternoon I am at my friend's house for their annual feast. After a sumptuous lunch as usual we go out into the garden and I find an effigy on fire. The smaller children are running around throwing little twigs at the burning man as he falls on his face.

"What is this?" I ask.

"Oh, it's nothing," says my friend, her face red with embarrassment. "I don't know what these kids are up to."

Just then one of her little cousins runs up to us and says, "We set fire to Pandit Nehru."

I cannot make any sense of it, and I feel deeply embarrassed. Our grandmothers are best friends, and our grandfathers rely upon each other. Pandit Nehru is a Kashmiri Brahmin just like us, so I cannot imagine what he must have done to deserve being set afire.

"Why?" I ask.

"He is the Prime Minister of India."

"Oh," I say, and to myself I say that it has nothing to do with us being friends. I could not have been quite ten years old and I went home bewildered and afraid. It was my first cognitive encounter with the menacing possibilities of hatred.

Like the ripples caused by a falling chinar leaf on the placid waters of our lakes political resentment creates a stir now and then in our life. The circles of water soon disappear into the nothingness from whence they came. But even though the leaves keep falling with increasing frequency, we naively prefer to believe that it is not inevitable that a frozen season will soon be upon our heels.

Most Kashmiris want a promise to be kept. They want their opinions on their political future to be polled. On the other hand, India has decided that since so many elections have taken place in the valley, it confirms the people's decision to be a part of India. These two ways of looking at the same facts are to fester and grow in the belly of Kashmir, and finally end up in a volcanic eruption that no one's prayers can avert.

We have managed to avert calamity so far, but no one can avert destruction if it is preceded by lack of wisdom. At night at home in my bed I remember the effigy burning and falling to the ground, facedown. I shudder because the cremation of a man standing up is a horrible sight to behold. It is too disturbing an experience to repeat to my family.

When Shivratri comes around in winter my Muslim friend

comes over for lunch as usual. Like so many other unpalatable things we have put the burning episode behind us. Shivratri is the most important festival for us and my friend honors our sentiments.

My friend is not the only Muslim who participates with us on this sacred day. The provisions for Shivratri, the pottery vessels, meats, fish, and other ritualistic items are all bought from Muslim traders. We are grown from the same seed on the same soil, and although Muslims have accepted Islam, they have supported our obsession for centuries as well.

Perhaps this is because Kashmir has been the center of Shaivite beliefs forever. We pandits know the mythology by heart. Shiva of the matted hair and live snake jewelry and ashes for talcum powder meditates atop a snow-clad mountain in a yogic pose, inanimate until the energizing Female awakens him. His neck is blue from the poison it has imprisoned, and his only garment is a loincloth of snow leopard skin. To Parvati he is the most desirable man she has ever seen. The Female is transfixed, this beloved daughter of a mountain king, and she cannot move or be moved.

"Cosmic forces are at work," says my mother, "they are just doing the dance of creation." Now that I am approaching a marriageable age my mother has firmly taken over the task of pushing me in the right direction. We are shelling peas and looking for little green worms in the pea pods. We do not consciously spend time together as mother and child, but the task of seeing me enter adulthood, initiating me into the dance steps is my mother's sole preoccupation now. She no longer accompanies my father on his postings, now she and my sister and little brother stay on in Kashmir most of the time. There is nothing more important for the mother of a post-pubescent girl than to collect her trousseau and then to keep watch over her and her dowry preparation.

"The king is enraged, how can his priceless daughter be given to a wandering ascetic with a begging bowl? He weeps and cries and rants and raves. He curses his wife for the way she has brought up their daughter." My mother is singing now as she deftly separates the peas and chucks them into a wicker basket from her mother's village.

I look at my mother. She narrates the story with extreme unction, as if she is gossiping about one of our relatives. I recognize some of her mother's phraseology, but I dare not question the authorship of the lyrical narrative. She has become a mother like her own, and when she sees me she sees herself and she is uncertain, I can tell. Will she be as able as her mother to reach me safely to my destiny? The song is not without purpose.

"But, Father," continues my mother, "he is the Divine One. See him with your true eyes, and your soul will know him." She sings the Kashmiri verses that soulfully encapsulate the whole affair as if it happened yesterday. I have no doubt that Shiva and Parvati speak fluent Kashmiri. She is enraptured every time she tells me this story. So am I.

"What happened?" I ask. I know, but like all the other stories she tells me I want to hear it again.

"What else? This was going to happen, nothing could stop this union of two halves which make a whole. Like all fathers the mountain king held the wedding as if nothing had happened, as if Shiva was the most eligible bachelor. She was his child, what could he do? What can any parent do?" She looks at me a trifle apprehensively. "When the bridegroom arrived sitting on a bull the relatives shrieked with laughter. But Parvati was the Goddess and her father knew that now. Her father married her off as he should and Shiva and Parvati set up house in the Himalayas."

Presumably this is where we found them and worshipped them. They belonged to us and we belonged to them.

But Shiva is unpredictable and he can turn everything to ashes just in the blink of his third eye. So we appease him by celebrating his marriage every year. As seductive as he was to the

Female, his attraction to Parvati must have been equally over-powering. He became a regular fellow, gave up his asceticism, threw off his snakes, his smoking pipes, and his ashes, and went in for a traditional wedding, with in-laws and receptions and feasts and banquets. This is the part we like, and we, being mortals, try to imitate the divine.

The image of Shiva, alternatively coifed, powdered, and perfumed, and clothed in minimalist style is not so odd to us. Kashmir is populated by Shiva-wannabes; in summer there is an influx of door-to-door ascetics from all over India heading for the phallic lingam in the Amarnath cave. They rattle dried gourds and cymbals at our gate and loudly invoke Shiva, and we give them alms, whether it's rice grains or lentils or fruits or money. We hurry inside the house afterward, primarily because the ascetics are barely clothed, and secondly because they seem to belong to another cosmos, and thirdly because strange stories surround them. When angered they can impale a person with their tridents and hurl the punctured body for hundreds of yards. We have also heard that when they reach Shiva's cave at Amarnath they meditate naked in the freezing temperatures wearing garlands around their erect penises.

As if in confirmation of our myth of finding the Divine Couple on our mountains, centuries ago a Muslim shepherd found a gigantic ice lingam in the Amarnath cave while taking shelter during a storm. The shepherd's descendants now receive a percentage of the temple income. Hindus, some even from the hot, tropical, and coastal South, trek through icy glaciers, and make the perilous climb to bathe at icy springs and pray at the cave as their forebears have done.

The presence of stone depictions of sexual intercourse in our temples does not embarrass us at all. The symbol has transcended the fact. The business of fertility and life is so vital that graphic representations of reproductive parts of our bodies and sexual activity go quite unnoticed. The most erotic stories we hear are those about our gods, but in our mortal world, romantic love is publicly expressed only through the fine arts. Kissing, or holding hands in public is simply not done, all these acts are considered superficial.

Shiva has devotees from the West as well, but these fans are only interested in copying his bad habits. We worship a hippie god, and so we don't worry about the white hippies who come to Kashmir to smoke pot and wander about without any clothes. Penniless foreigners with matted blond hair and cheap jewelry sit Shiva-like by the lakeside, staring into nothingness with their vacuous drugged eyes. The hippies become just another item in our collection of strange people.

What if I were to present the family with my male inanimate half from one of these dirty white men with yellow hair, and look to completing our cosmos? It's just a thought, and anyway we have heard that the hippies never bathe and stink to high heaven. I search my mother's eyes for answers to these unasked questions.

She hastily concludes the love story by saying, "Only Parvati could recognize Shiva under all the ash and the snakes. No ordinary mortal can see the Lord."

We are done shelling the peas. A marriage that breaks all the rules is only for the gods.

And anyway, marriage is ultimately all about children.

Infants are reared with great care and fear. Nothing is expected of young children, and no parent is too proud to go begging for his child. When we eat, grown-ups look the other way for fear of casting an evil eye. When we play or accomplish great things no one talks about it for the same reason. But we only have to see their eyes to know their joy.

Much is left unspoken. The spoken word is a force to be reckoned with, reverberating forever in the cosmos, causing all kinds of repercussions. This is because words have a deity all their own, an unrelenting goddess under whose regime a sound once uttered cannot die but goes around and around, doing good or bad, depending on its nature. Children are especially vulnerable to bad thoughts and words.

When children come out of nursling clothes, they wear pants with holes cut out in strategic places to drop unwanted liquid and solids. They carry on unself-consciously, until suddenly ashamed and then they run for the privacy of the bathroom. Then the children can be taken everywhere, still holding an adult's hand. Eventually the children come out of the *paridaeza,* the charmed enclosure, the paradise of home, and head for school. Some go to government schools with vernacular instruction, but my siblings and I, children and grandchildren of Western-educated people, head across the river to a private convent school.

Our school is housed in a turn-of-the-century brick building. Atop the convent school's imposing brick clock tower shines a golden cross which you can see from miles away. We are going to be taught in English, still the language of the ruling classes in a free, Babel-like, India. Shyamji arranges for one of the boatmen at the dock, Habiba, to ferry us to and from school every day until we graduate high school. The boat is a small, flat-bottomed *shikara,* whose roof is a reed mat held up by wooden poles. There is comfortable cushioned seating for four inside the boat, but the more daring among us cross the river standing up, holding one of the poles. The oars are heart-shaped, as they have always been.

The convent emphasizes history, geography, literature, and music, and its library is richly stocked with books on these subjects.

I remember that the library hour was the highlight of my school day. But we are getting a Western education. We read Lewis Carroll, Robert Louis Stevenson, Dickens. Our history books make sure that the Tudors and the Stuarts are not forgotten. We sing "The Last Rose of Summer" to music played on the piano, and participate in lots of Western music concerts and theater. We still wander about in parts of the British Empire, read about Australian trees, or kookaburras, or Burma, or dream of African safaris. But we are hardly taught anything about our own pristine surroundings, and our Himalayan flora and fauna. Our history of India is supplemented by revisionist explanations offered by the slightly embarrassed Irish nuns in a post-independence world. We know the truth from home and let it pass.

One of the nuns is preoccupied with another British colony. She plies us with Negro songs like "Old Folks at Home (Swanee River)" and "My Old Kentucky Home." We read *Uncle Tom's Cabin, Hiawatha,* and all those *Little Men* and *Women* books; we admire Abraham Lincoln. We are not surprised that Englishmen have created mayhem in another country. My grandfather says that Paul Robeson is the finest singer in the world; he loves "Ol' Man River." I think his admiration had a lot to do with the success of a black man in a racist time. We are told nothing about contemporary America.

At the private school we are doomed to a lower level of math and science than our old-city relatives who study at government schools. There if you don't know mathematics you don't know anything. Our negligence of science and mathematics at the convent will show us up in our later lives when semiconductors and biotechnology and graduates of our vernacular schools will rule the waves.

We don't know it, but we are regressing into the past, reading ourselves into obsolescence at the expensive convent school, preparing to work in a British India that no longer exists. The nuns teach us everything they know, and they give us our money's worth. If our classes are outdated it is because we are getting what we have asked and paid for, and we still crave a colonial certification.

✻✻✻

Our relatives are gleefully contemptuous of our education and spare no opportunity to deride the high fees and low returns. They live in the old city alongside the second, third, fourth, fifth, sixth, and seventh bridges on the river Jhelum. They don't say so openly, but they consider us who live close to the first bridge and the government buildings still enslaved to the British and their ways, now considered artificial in post-independence India. It makes no difference to anyone that our nuns are Irish. We don't know that the Irish hate the English with a vehemence that we have never allowed ourselves to feel. We think they are all the same, all look the same, and some are better and definitely better-looking than others.

It is the lunch hour at the convent school. The main building is surrounded by extensive acreage divided in half by a narrow avenue of poplar trees. Between the two rows of poplar trees are wooden benches. From these benches as we eat lunch we can see the oak trees that shelter the nun's residential area. We can see the terraced frontage of the school complete with manicured hedges and birdbaths. We can also see the main entrance to the school; it has a circular glass window with parquet panes through which we can see the grand piano in the parlor.

When we come for admission to the convent school we enter through the main entrance and are thereafter forbidden from using that entrance. Perhaps that is why it is so sparkling clean all the time.

Once we go inside the school is built cloister-style and contains a beautiful geometric garden with garden paths and arbors. For a convent it is a highly romantic place, with love seats under the arbors. The nuns advise us to keep God in our hearts when we fall in love, and we don't have the heart to tell them our gods are up to all kinds of hanky-panky. The convent is not a place where you can talk about a phallic symbol as an object of worship, although by the time we are at the high school level some of us are taking the first steps on that pilgrimage.

The convent is a private school for mostly Hindu and Muslim girls whose families can afford the fees. What better place to educate girls than an all-girls school run by strict Irish nuns brandishing hard wooden rulers? But every class has a couple or so boys who are special cases, so we are not entirely free of danger. The Irish priests who run the boys' school a mile away also come over to visit our nuns.

Almost all of the girls at the convent school are in love with one priest in particular, whom I remember as a Peter O'Toole look-alike. Our city has three cinema halls that show mainly Indian films but matinees and evening shows are for "English films." Fortunately all three theaters are within walking distance of our house. The explicit kissing and implied sex in the "English films" has sent our inexperienced minds on a rampage because we have not even seen anyone holding hands in public in real life. The only men we have seen kissing are "English" and the presence of a good-looking Irish priest sends the thrill of double jeopardy down our high school spines. We dare not say it aloud even to each other, it must be a sin to think carnally of a priest, and these thoughts are left at the convent school gate when we go home every day, as though they might be discovered even though tucked away inside the head. It is better to forget because if we do not we may say something and all will be lost because we can never take it back again.

I have a feeling that the nuns feel the same way as we do about the priest. It is impossible not to, particularly when Father comes tearing down the driveway on his motorcycle with his blond hair flying in the face of all self-control. He is wearing khaki shorts and when he gets off the bike and walks in tall, lanky steps into the nun's parlor, some inner thigh is in evidence. The boarders tell us that the nuns serve him tea and special cakes baked by the servants, but the boarders complain that they don't get any of it. This story is difficult to reconcile with the fact that every Sunday the nuns assiduously distribute dry milk powder and other essential provisions to the river boatmen who have pursued the same livelihood century after century. When we feel under the weather at school the nuns rush us off to rest in the infirmary and wake us up with tea and brown bread.

I envy the boarders' institutional food, as bad as they make it out to be, and the predictability and discipline of living in a regimented world because I live at home. The alternative is appealing only because I don't have it. The one time I have doubts about exchanging one for the other is when the boarders tell me that they are never warm enough in the winter.

The nuns advocate brandy when the boarders have a cold. They themselves imbibe dark brown medical liquids after dinner sometimes, brought to them in tiny glasses on a tray by a faithful convent retainer. The glasses are covered with a lace doily held down by blue glass beads woven into the edge. For us Kashmiris alcohol is something men do outside the home and it is not a subject for discussion except when things get out of hand. In our neighborhood there is one person, the gentlest of men, who often comes home well past midnight and we all know about it. When he lets himself in, the steel garden gates scrape the granite walk, then its heavy latch clicks loudly into place, and his return reverberates through the quiet night. We never complain about the disturbance; it is already too shameful and painful for our neighbors.

The nuns may be liberal with brandy, but they would surely break our finger bones with their long hard wooden rulers if we smoked. This they have in common with my grandmother for whom a cigarette is equally out of the question, rather like fowl and shallots and china in her seemingly arbitrary caste system. She will never touch it; it is a foreign object, unclean, made by unclean hands, and only bad women and men smoke cigarettes anyway.

One of my friends comes to school one day with unmoving symmetrical breasts and we discover bras. We are quite relieved because we have not told anyone, but life has become quite unbearable for us, particularly during sports. So, as grim as the idea of elastic and hooks and straps replacing complete freedom is, the relief makes it all worthwhile. Soon we are comparing brassiere sizes.

We don't worry much about boys, except for a crush here and there, but we never admit it, and we know it as gospel truth that a girl must always be impossible to approach until marriage. This is one of the areas of complete agreement between the Kashmiris and the nuns. It heightens our sense of self-worth and power to be able to torture a boy by appearing uninterested. In any case it means nothing. We are all going to have arranged marriages.

We groom ourselves seriously now. We learn the fine and painful art of threading our facial hair, and progress from talcum powder to cologne and from utilitarian underclothes to lacy bras and panties. The tailor with the pencil behind his ear and measuring tape in hand is asked by us to take tighter measurements for our shirts and skirts. A good businessman, the tailor quietly obliges with an absolutely straight face. He has been our family tailor for decades and he has seen us as infants, but now he is our confidant. The nuns don't mind tight-fitting clothes, or our legs showing all the way up to our knees, but even a sliver of upper arm or midriff showing causes them to hyperventilate.

My relatives from the old city look unbelievingly at my legs and ask my mother why I must go to school naked. At least I wear underclothes, I think to myself; you are the ones who are naked. It's a delicate balance, who is naked and who is not. None of it seems to make any sense to me at this point in my life where my face is overwhelmed by a plague of pimples. My mother says that my pimples are like blemishes on the moon. She says that I am like a peacock, exquisite except for my feet, which should be on a villager. Whenever she looks at me I feel fragmented into items of perfection and defect; she can never see me as a whole.

Meanwhile at lunchtime at school we chase puffs of cotton from the poplar trees. I see old Mohammedu opening up the lunch basket he has brought for us from home and spreading out a blue and white tablecloth on the wooden bench. He is a short, darkish man with a skullcap and a wise old face, and his back is bent a little with age. He knows the lyrics of most of our folk songs and sings under his breath as he sets out cream-colored Bengal Potteries' plates and cutlery with cream-colored imitation bone handles on the tablecloth. Then he pulls a hot, four-tiered lunchbox out of an insulated aluminum container. We are ravenously hungry. Mohammedu sets out rice and lamb and a vegetable curry for us, and some red radishes picked from our kitchen garden. I love the unreal red color and the astringent crisp taste of the radish, eaten while still with its bright green leaves attached.

There is some yogurt, only my sister willingly eats it here at school although at home my brother and I are forced to eat some. We are incredulous when told by the boarders that the nuns don't touch or serve yogurt at the convent. We are surprised that they have not as a result all shriveled up with boils and blisters from body heat. Food is either heat or cold producing, and you have to be careful how you balance everything, what you eat in a particular season or when you feel a certain way. We did not have a guidebook, but by the time we left for college, we had formed a subconscious chart of foods and their properties. A meal without yogurt at some juncture during the day is inconceivable. The boarders say that the nuns serve them a stew of lamb and potatoes with rice every day.

"At least we get rice," says one boarder, native of a valley of green rice fields and yellow mustard seed flowers. Her hands are tucked firmly into a red worsted wool blazer with a pocket emblazoned with the school logo which she wears over a bottle-green tunic, and a white shirt and red tie and belt. It always seemed to me that boarders missed their food more than anything else.

Mohammedu supervises our lunch and we obey his instructions; he has the power of a parent over us. Our best friends are there as well eating lunch, and like us rushing through so that we can play in the little time remaining in our break. We mainly run around playing catch. Some of the girls who have been the focus of boy attention huddle together and giggle; sometimes they play with the rest of us. We console ourselves by feeling sorry for the girls because of the retribution they are surely bound to receive for having boys on their brain. Anyway we would rather run around madly chasing or being chased.

Then, a girl from faraway Bombay with mysterious family circumstances joins the school. We have never seen the sea, and she says she can see the sea from her apartment in Bombay. We have many-storied homes, but no one lives in apartments. She looks too mature to be in our grade. Her father looks too young and distant. The mother looks too voluptuous for anyone's good; her breasts want to fall out of her blouse and her lipstick strays way beyond her God-given lips.

The Bombay mother and daughter are so close they could be sisters. We do not have that kind of equality at home. When my mother discovered a bottle of red nail polish in my clothes it went flying out of my upstairs bedroom window down into the vegetable patch directly below. When I ran to look down from the window I could see the crimson culprit stuck in the mud, shining among the aubergines and the aubergine blossoms.

We did not exist as co-women, my mother and I, just as mother and child. Neither of us wanted to acknowledge anything in the other that smacked of sexuality. Nor did anyone else. It all seemed to be silently understood, fed with songs and stories, kept in the unspoken realm.

At school all of us naturally want to be friends with the girl from the sea. We cannot determine her religion from her name, it sounds newfangled, and she does nothing to illuminate us further on the subject. She laughs when she talks about her escapades and the boys in Bombay. To her it does not matter that the word will get out and that matchmakers will stop coming to her house, or that relatives will take her off the list of desirable girls. She does not come from a valley where everyone can see the boundaries from home.

Bombay sounds like a vast city of freedom, wanton lifestyles, and anonymity. It is a foreign country to us; the buildings have flat roofs, while our houses have gables so that the snow can slide down in the winter. The Bombay girl, she misses her seafood, with its strong smells, its real sea flavor. Our sweet river fish smell and taste bland to her. We have never had seafood in our lives. She knows all the latest dances and she wears sleeveless blouses under the school tunic, but undoubtedly the nuns, in their irrational way, will soon put a stop to that.

As expected, they give her a smart little whack with the ruler on her upper arm and say, "Young lady, go home, buy six inches of material and stitch it on to your blouse." The girl from Bombay adds sleeves to her blouse, and the reprimand restores the balance for us somewhat, but not for long. In the girls' lavatory she tells us that she can go swimming even when she has her periods, and we know what that means. Her triumph over her new surroundings is complete when she gives us the added information that she smokes. We are in complete adulation of this reckless girl. She looks at us as if we are country bumpkins, which is what we are, and we all want to invite her home.

Between ourselves, it gives us the shudders. At home women still talk about grooms who look for a spot of blood on the marriage bed to make sure that they are the first. In some of the rural areas they tie tiny bells on the drawstring of the bride's trousers or petticoats and listen at the door to make sure that what should be done is being done.

Suddenly in the middle of our lunchtime idylls, a large nun emerges in the distance and stands at the side entrance to the school. A silver cross dangles on a rosary chain down her prodigious side, one hand is on her belt, the other hand rings a bell; she has come out to herd us in. At the mere sight of the white summer habit old Mohammedu bursts into a long nonsensical sentence. He thinks his mutterings sound like English and often has us giggling hysterically when he "talks" to us in English. Now he has his own little giggle as he talks to our nun from a safe distance. She cannot hear him and little does she know that the hunchbacked little man is engaged in a conversation with her. Only when he has finished does he pack our plates, the hot case, the tablecloth, and the cutlery into the basket and go home.

We line up, grade-wise, and file past the nun who is picking her teeth—must be the lamb from the stew, I think. Just before I enter the cloister I turn to see old Mohammedu disappear along with other servants up the long driveway of the school. They will walk toward the dock where they will take a boat across the river and go home. Sometimes I wish I could go home with him and run up the porch to my grandparents. If I suggest that, and off and on I do, he sternly refuses and tells me to run along and go back to class so that I do not bring shame upon my family. Honor is everything to us.

Our servants have a superior air about them; their wards have saintlike English teachers who never get married. Moreover, we eat with forks and knives at school, on untouchable modern china plates. At home we eat from metal plates with our fingers while sitting on the floor, as does the entire local population, whether Muslim or Hindu. At night Mohammedu brings huge terra-cotta basins of salted hot water into the family room and washes and pumices our feet before we go to bed. In winter this prevents chilblains.

I rather enjoy going to school. I love the fact that at school our desks are neat, the glass is clean, and the floors are like mirrors. Everything wooden in our classroom is polished to a shine with shoe polish, which we bring from home. Compared to the disarray of my grandfather's carefree house, I like the fact that I find my scissors and rulers and paints and pencils where I leave them the previous day.

If we ever do anything worthwhile the nuns will take us to the chapel as a treat. The chapel is always a little dark, but it is quiet there, and the holy water smells of some familiar flower. We take the whole exercise of kneeling before the altar and making the sign of the cross to heart because of a rumor that Mother Peter has seen the devil and fought him. I never quite know what to make of that story except that she has physically seen a little bloody-eyed horned creature with a tail and a trident and sent him packing with one of her stout stockinged legs. In any event, Mother looks completely in control thereafter, and very cheerful at that, and it makes us feel important to be joined with the nuns in protecting the convent. We do everything to discourage another visitation.

We have no single entity equivalent to the devil in Hinduism. Our creatures of the netherworld are a different kettle of fish, and have been vanquished in intellectual, spiritual, and physical battles with our mythical heroes. We have been spared the inconvenience. All we have to be careful of is us, and what we might do in a moment of lack of wisdom, a state that always precedes destruction.

At the convent, though, Satan seems determined to trip us up and we take him very seriously. We fortify ourselves with holy pictures and holy medals given to us by visiting church dignitaries. We prepare for Christmas with the same feverishness that the nuns do, as if it is the very purpose of the entire school year. The best part for me is reinterpreting old Christmas cards in watercolor and gouache. The nuns proudly send our cards to church officials around the world. We paint furiously, and eventually master the essential ingredients for a Christmas card: holly leaves and berries in a beautiful red and green juxtaposition, angels, an archetypal spruce, calligraphy, and bells, and musical notes flowing out of improbable places.

The nuns combine art and religion into one greatly uplifting experience for all of us before sending us home for our long winter break that lasts until March. Later it will take quite an effort to shake off the Western liturgical quality in my artwork and replace it with our liturgical art of well-endowed women with promising rounded pelvic areas.

Our devotion to Christian art and prayers has nothing to do with the pursuit of our own religion. We do not burden the nuns with our own beliefs; they seem not to have any curiosity about our religious life. In fact, we strongly suspect that they might be quite put out if we enlightened them about our theology. Can we really tell them about all the raw fish and meat our deities consume on an annual basis? We just stick to enjoying school and leave Christianity at the convent and our religion at home.

After ten years of school we matriculate from the convent. The nuns give us a farewell party and don't mind when we show up with lipstick. They allow us to play gramophone records in the auditorium and dance the latest dances, which we have learned from the Bombay girl. They watch us from the side, hands folded at the stomach, smiling like parents. It is sad to leave these pious, strong women, but we are now all about thirteen years old and are straining to be a little freer. We look forward to attending college, if only for the freedom it is sure to bring after the unrelenting supervision of the nuns. But first we must clear the qualifying entrance examinations. The nuns march us to our examination hall, a rare excursion out of the cloister for them. They enjoy it, though, quietly telling us a joke or two en route to boost our morale for the tests.

After passing our examinations we head for the one women's college in town. This is the same college to which my aunts went, and where my grandfather and my youngest aunt and, for a while, my sister taught. My mother was tutored at home. Her parents were always two steps more conservative than my father's family.

The college building is a gothic stone structure. It used to be the palace for royal widows. Perhaps in recognition of the original inhabitants of the building, the college is only for women, though as in the past men walk or drift in and out in different capacities. At the women's college we feel completely in control of our situation. Our eyes survey the men as they enter our domain and walk up the crescent drive to the college porch. Once they enter the college gates, which are guarded by the only seven-foot man I ever saw in Kashmir, the men lose the poise they enjoy in the outside world. This is a woman's world and they know they are being appraised, so some walk briskly, some boldly, taking in the females, some hesitantly, and some with their eyes glued to the road.

When young men enter the college gates and no teacher is within sight or earshot, we serenade them with love songs. We do not know if the visitors are married or single, and we don't care. We don't intend anything to come of it because we are all going to have arranged marriages. Sometimes a professor catches us and gives us a broad smile and walks on. Some teachers are less charitable and make a mental note, putting us down as promiscuous, and it takes forever for them to change their mind.

We may or may not work after college, but we will all get married after our parents find us a husband. There is always the odd girl or two who will defy all laws of probability and find a decent boy on her own, let him court her on the sly, and then marry him. We have not had any boyfriends, so the prospect of any fairly pleasant-looking young man with a decent lifestyle holds romantic possibilities, none of which are usually pursued by us. Such ventures more often than not bring nothing but shame and loss of honor; it is much safer to let our parents do the research and narrow down the choices.

My mother has gradually started preparing and arranging for my marriage. She was married at fourteen and has resentfully, but not admittedly, accepted the idea that she may have to wait several years before she sees me as a bride.

The royal ladies for whom our college building was first constructed are long since gone, but I am acutely aware of their presence. It is as if they still live there; it is as if I can actually see them. The widowed queens and princesses are a mixed lot, old and young, happy and sad, all husbandless. They wear white, and I can see through them. Some of them have lips stained red from the walnut bark with which they clean their teeth. Their hair flows freely and softly, as if it has just been left to dry after being washed with water from soaked olives and soap-nut berries. These women live the leisure of nothingness in death as in life. There are no lustful half-closed royal eyes for which the women might occasionally be called upon to weave their long hair into intricate coiffures. Even the sparse couplings that each of the many wives live for have vanished with widowhood. Some are content and some are hungry, and they look at us with vacant eyes.

I can swear that the royal females look at us from behind corners, or from the far end of our long corridors as we rush from class to class, carrying our books. Most of them must have been mothers. Did they leave their children behind at the grand palace?

The widows from the royal family were ousted from the main palace after their husbands died, and sent to this comfortable but modest bungalow to serve out the rest of their lives. We do not have a tradition of women jumping into funeral pyres after their husbands in our valley, and we are horrified when we hear about this happening in other parts of India. It is absurd that any mother would send her daughter to die with a dead man.

The palace widows may have escaped self-immolation, but they were accursed women nevertheless. What else is a woman who does not have the good fortune to die naturally or by accident while still married? But a widowed prince is just a new marriage waiting to happen, whoever the lucky woman might be. The selection of a second wife is easier; a lot is overlooked. The main college building has a cloister behind it as well, a big square garden with rooms and verandahs on all sides of it. The main building is double-storied, but the three sides of the cloister are single-storied rooms, one for each widow or concubine. Students boarding at the college now live in these rooms.

It is a great contrast that enthusiasm and fulfillment are found by the students in that palace of purposeless women. The exorcism of any doom lingering in our future is achieved single-handedly by the principal, a brave Muslim woman. The descendent of fearless mountain nomads, she wants to make real women out of us; she cannot abide irresponsibility and giggling. Our principal is a statuesque, handsome woman. She has sturdy ankles as well. There is something of an oak tree about her, except that she can be disarmingly attractive when she wants to be.

The principal of the Women's College is a compelling mentor who scales issues that angels might have had doubts about. She is unmarried, and does exactly as she pleases, with a hereditary surefootedness, and with great poise and sometimes charm. She aims to make each successive batch of students that enter her college gates into confident, capable women and we have the feeling that we can achieve anything. The credo of the college is up for all to see, just below the name of the college on the signboard above the main entrance: "Light to Enlighten." We are expected to bring up the next generation the way we have been taught. There is no doubt that we are training to ride a different tiger from our mothers.

The college is set on well-kept lawns and gardens, and a portion of the palace compound has been converted to a sports field, which is busy in spring, summer, and fall with athletics. Instructors from the navy, air force, and army teach us to march and drill. We do not want to join the forces, but a brief encounter with volunteer training during the Kabaili raid has introduced Kashmiri women to the army life. My eldest aunt, an adventurous young woman, even took my grandmother for firing practice when the volunteer army was in full swing. Tulli eventually found her army niche knitting socks for all the young lads on the front. Our principal made sure that her own experience of marching, physical training, and discipline became part of our college curriculum.

To us who have never seen the sea the navy man is the main attraction. His white uniform with the beret and its ribbon hanging down his neck, the sailor's collar on his white shirt, and his crisply starched white shorts all make him quite appealing. He is from a different geography, a part of India where it is never cold.

Going to the convent school I had crossed the river every day in Habiba's boat, which was furnished with plump red and yellow cushions. As the boat slid through the water, the other bank and the tall clock tower of the convent school were in full view. Habiba the shikara wallah saw me graduate from kindergarten to middle school to matriculation and eventually bid farewell when I left the convent school for the college, which was on my side of the river.

The ocean is completely outside our reckoning. In the valley we can see our limits from our homes and we can always tell where we are and where we are going. The idea of pulling away from a well-known shore with no land in sight, with only the ocean and the sky sharing the secrets of the impending voyage is frightening, to say the least.

Everything in Srinagar is within walking distance. My college is around the corner from where I live, and I come home frequently for a quick lunch, sometimes with friends. It is wonderful to have the comfort of my family house a couple of minutes away from my college.

As secure as we feel at home, college has undoubtedly become the most important part of the day for me and my friends. The college building is a bit cavernous and forbidding when seen from the outside, but for us it has opened up an exciting world and we cannot keep away. It is a gathering place within whose high walls we girls shall make the move into adulthood together. The college halls and corridors are coldly luxurious, although wainscoting and chandeliers and ceilings trimmed with intricate molding give the interiors a slight touch of warmth. We attend classes in what must once have been grand rooms and anterooms, all severe but unmistakably royal. Some of the original carpets and rococo furniture and paintings are still in faded evidence, bits and pieces forgotten and left behind, like the women. As we rehearse plays or musicals, or hold debates and seminars in the stone palace we are overwhelmed by the fate of our predecessors and determine that we will not be so easily discarded.

The widow's palace, which is how the college is still referred to, has become a beehive of women's emancipation, abuzz with studies, classes, books, plays, song, dance, fashion, and debates.

A wide variety of courses are offered in the syllabus. The girls who have taken Domestic Science treat us to their weekly experiments, delicious concoctions from their "labs." I am fortunate enough to have an aunt, Shakti, in this field and for her I am a more than eager guinea pig. She is named after two critical elements of our existence: Shakti the female energy of the cosmos, and *takil* or spindle, which is what she was called at home. Shakti is since gone, taken young from her children and a loving family she left behind, but I still continue to make the cauliflower and lamb curry she once tried out on me. I could never get it out of my mind.

Other girls pursue physics and chemistry and work on "labs" that do not promise such instant gratification. We liberal arts types cannot understand why anyone would want to study mathematics and science if they don't have to, but some of our friends happily spend hours in foul-smelling laboratories.

My circle of friends and I are heavily into theater, we put on Wilde, Molière, Shakespeare, Hindi and Urdu plays, Kashmiri operas and drama, and my favorite, comedies. My youngest aunt, a professor of English at my college and an esteemed successor to my grandfather, is the courageous director of many an ambitious production and our chief enthusiast. She leaves no stone unturned to stage as authentic a production as she can. The costumes we wear are painstakingly reproduced from pictures shown to the college tailor. But underneath the tailcoats, makeup, and wigs, all the male protagonists, such as the Imaginary Invalid, Hamlet, and even the all-important Earnest, are females at the core. I must admit that I enjoyed plays in our native languages the most, particularly the comedies. There is no joke as good as a joke in the vernacular.

One of our oft-requested theatrical productions is a contemporary Kashmiri opera called *Bombur Yemberzal* or *The Narcissus and the Bumble Bee,* which celebrates Kashmir as a free garden where a thousand flowers bloom. So popular is the opera that phrases from the libretto find their way into our language almost immediately. Play practice provides us with an ironclad excuse to cut classes and have a good time, our truancy occasionally enhanced with snacks provided courtesy of the college. It is a measure of the vision of our principal that she considers this aspect of our education also to be vital, though she did expect a first-rate production at the end of it all. We rarely disappointed.

When we perform *Bombur Yemberzal* it is a visual delight. I can see the chorus of singers dressed in white robes and gold belts, their faces flushed because they are on stage for the first time. They are also wearing makeup for the first time, and they love it; they look beautiful and life is promising. Each girl in the chorus represents a flower that she wears in profusion on her head. Halfway through the opera the chorus presciently asks the rapt audience, "Will not our garden be laid to waste by the seasons?"

As I look out at the audience I see my grandparents in the front row, as always.

Hardly any national or international dignitary visiting Kashmir misses a trip to our college.

In 1960, the very first year of our college career, the dramatic society puts on *Malini,* a play by the Nobel laureate Rabindranath Tagore. The chief guest is Pandit Jawaharlal Nehru, the first prime minister of India, a native son of Kashmir. On this trip he is accompanied by his only child, Indira Gandhi, and her two sons. Just before curtain's up, Pandit Nehru suddenly stands and a hush descends on the auditorium. Has something gone wrong? We hold our breath as Nehru walks back down the aisle looking for someone. Moments later he returns with his petite and unprepossessing cabinet colleague who had been asked to sit among the not-so-VIP in the rear of the auditorium. Someone vacates a seat and Lal Bahadur Shastri sits down next to Nehru, whom he would succeed after his death. On Nehru's other side sits Indira, and next to her, her two sons from her marriage to Feroze Gandhi, whose Zoroastrian ancestors came from Persia. Little did we know that we had four prime ministers of India in our audience that day.

After the play is over we are presented to our special guests who, being polite, compliment us quite liberally.

My best friend played my mother in the play, even though I was twice her size. She and I were prone to escapades, mostly at her instigation. So, when she showed up at twilight next day to pick me up and said, "Come along, we are going to meet Pandit Nehru," I had a gnawing suspicion we were going to do exactly that.

"What do you mean?" I asked anyway.

"Pandit Nehru loved the play and I am sure he would like to meet us again," she said. Once she made up her mind, there was nothing to do but follow her.

The Prime Minister of India was in Kashmir to rest and recuperate in the gardens of the Royal Spring of Chashma Shahi, just like the rulers of another age. When the world was too much with Pandit Nehru, this was his favorite holiday. He was staying at the Government Guesthouse, a graceful structure built near a cluster of ancient chinars. The gardens start at the spring on the hilltop and flow down in formal terraces all the way to the bottom of the hill.

The two of us approached Chashma Shahi in my friend's car, driven by her chauffeur. At the barricades outside the guesthouse, we were stopped abruptly by security. At this point I timidly suggested that we return home. But another police officer who had come to our college play with the Prime Minister recognized us, and not wanting to take any chances he waved us on. My friend was armed with a notebook for autographs, which she had grabbed from home, and a camera, which she handed to me.

After all the official visitors left we were ushered in to meet Pandit Nehru after being given strict instructions to stay for only a couple of minutes. Before we knew what was happening we found ourselves face to face with our most celebrated national figure. Pandit Nehru looked unwell and tired. He was sitting on a garden chair, dressed informally, but impeccably, his signature red rose buttonholed in the lapel of his sleeveless jacket. Behind him stood Mrs. Gandhi, one hand protectively on his chair. Behind her, looking down at us from the balcony of the guesthouse, were her two sons, Rajeeva and Sanjay, who were roughly our age. My friend and I were stunned by our proximity to the "royal family," as they were sometimes called.

Then we heard Nehru say, "So what have you prepared for me?"

My friend and I shook our heads in speechless dismay; we had never imagined we would actually have a private audience, least of all be within handshaking distance with Pandit Nehru. Our tongues became firmly glued to the roof of our mouths.

"What is your greatest ambition?" Nehru asked, to help us recover.

We must have looked as if we were about to pass out because Mrs. Gandhi smiled and asked us if we would like a lime juice drink. In a dying gesture my friend thrust her autograph book into Pandit Nehru's hand, and he opened what turned out to be the family laundry book!

It seems surreal now but Pandit Nehru, the hero of our freedom movement, read aloud, "Two pajamas—Papaji, three shirts . . ." Both father and daughter burst out laughing. But he autographed the notebook, a thoroughly amused look on his face, and we survived the mortification because they were both so gracious. Perhaps they were grateful for the comic relief my friend and I provided after their meetings with Kashmiri leaders. The political situation in our state was acquiring a somber tone. Those who knew him said Nehru looked vulnerable for the first time, but my friend and I were electrified by his personality. It was a singular morning, and when we went home we were completely under the spell of Pandit Jawaharlal Nehru.

Four years later, in 1964, the principal of our college tearfully called an assembly to honor the passing of her hero, one of the greatest icons of Indian history. Pandit Nehru was second only to Mahatma Gandhi in securing the freedom of our nation from the British. My friends and I led the college girls on a march through the main street of Srinagar. It was the least we could do to honor the most outstanding Kashmiri in recent history. We called assembly at college and sent everyone home to bring symbolic black scarves to wear for the procession. The girls returned within the hour after dispersal, and we formed a parade line four to a row inside the college gates; there were about twelve hundred of us. Then Longman, as we called our tall gatekeeper, threw open the doors and we marched out shouting slogans in memory of Nehru. Our military training was obvious in the smart turnout we made that day.

More then thirty years later my daughter would call me excitedly from Smith College to say that she had found the newspaper photograph in the archives at her school library.

We had to send everyone home from college for black scarves because our uniform at college was white shirts and pants over which we wore long white scarves. The ensemble was called *salwar kameez dupatta*. Some of the Muslim girls from the inner city arrived at college wearing a *burqa* over their clothes, a tipto-toe black veil with beguiling lacework at the eyes. They religiously wore the burqa en route to the college, only to throw it in the cloakroom once they passed the gates. Eventually, most of the girls threw off the burqa at home and went on to become doctors, lawyers, engineers, scientists, professors, musicians, and housewives and mothers.

The widows cannot believe their ghostly eyes at the metamorphosis under way in their vacated home. We do not talk about the ladies, though their specters haunt the college. How can we forget them? But no connection can be made between unmarried girls and widows; it's bad enough that we study in a house of ill-fated women. Our families, fearful at heart about possible curse contamination, are nonetheless prepared to risk the unknown for our education. So, after making a few appropriate noises initially, no one brings up the subject of the auspices of our college again.

This acceptance by old-fashioned families is definitely facilitated by the fact that the college is entirely subsidized by the government. Education from nursery to university is free in our state. As a result, unlike the private convent school, our college is completely democratic. We have class fellows from different backgrounds; some of our parents cannot read or write and some of our parents are professors.

One day a girl sits next to me in class, she has a round face and her eyes are a soft brown. Her hair is parted in the middle, and she wears it in a plastic barrette at the back of her head. Her name is Izmat, which means honor, and she is the shawl peddler's daughter. Izmat is an avid reader and attends literature classes, although she has science subjects. She comes from a government school and lives in the inner city. Her father was right; not only is she smarter than her brothers, she is much smarter than most of us, and she runs rings around the teaching staff. She talks a lot like her father, and like him she is full of fun. Izmat lives up to her name and brings home honor every time examination results are announced or a debate is to be won. I miss her when she leaves for the medical college a few miles away, but we continue to be friends.

In summer the college camps up in the mountains and these excursions are the first time some of the inner-city girls, both Hindu and Muslim, have ever been away from their homes. The parents of these girls allow them to go on these trips only because they have tremendous faith in our iconoclastic principal. At night we light a bonfire, and sing Kashmiri folk songs or Indian film songs or tell ghost stories. One year we camp at Pahalgam, where pilgrims on the great pilgrimage to the ice-phallus shrine of Amarnath take their first break.

As you approach Pahalgam you can hear the deafening roar of the Liddar rolling down from the mountains, rushing over huge rocks. The valley is set perfectly, as if by design, below mountains covered with pine forests. Every day of the camp we explore Pahalgam on foot or on horseback, depending on the distance from the camp. A couple of ponies accompany us, carrying our lunch and tea-making equipment; tea always has to be freshly made, if we can manage it. We light a fire with kindling and small logs in an impromptu stove made of stones and set a pot on it. As the water boils it soaks in all the smoke from the mountain firewood. I thought I would never be able to taste that lovely smoky tea again until a friend presented me with a tin of Lapsang Souchong from Harrod's. One thing you can say with certainty about the British, if there was gold hidden in a colonial rock, they would market it.

After a long trek on a hot day we walk back down the mountainside toward the river. There we take off our shoes and sit on the sun-warmed rocks with our feet in icy cold water. Once rested, we start the uphill hike back to our camp, which is on another mountain.

One of our treks takes us through a village where the schoolmaster is teaching a class of small boys and girls. They are out in the open, in the sun, making good use of the all too brief mountain summer. The children's cheeks are red from the sun, the wind, the good food, and the outdoor life they lead. As we go by they stop studying and turn around to stare at us. We are city dwellers and they watch us mischievously and laugh at us. They see city folks so rarely that we are as good as foreigners to them. As we walk past, one of them mischievously shouts, "Long live Pakistan." They all laugh together.

The teacher asks them to be quiet and they begin to recite their lessons again, moving back and forth in unison, thin sing-song voices fading as we move out of earshot. Extraterritorial loyalty exists in some parts of the valley, we all know that. We don't talk much about it, but like a subterranean rumble it grows all the while.

Back at the college camp we sit outside in the sun and watch the gypsies come down the mountains. During the day the sun is so bright that our noses start to peel with sunburn. The gypsy women bring us rare fruits, and mozzarella-like stretchable buffalo milk cheese which only they can make. Intrepid foot soldiers of precipitous altitudes, they are also purveyors of wild vegetables and mushrooms which they alone can find; we do not usually try to climb that high. At night an eerie calm descends on Pahalgam; electricity is practically unavailable, and everything is silent except for the river, which sounds even more powerful and majestic at night. Inspired by shadows cast by the bonfire and the silent mountains we like to scare each other to death.

One evening Roxanna, whose father is an employee in the forest department of the government, tells us the scariest tale. Her great-grandfather knew a forest ranger who was posted to Kishtwar, a miniature valley also called Small Kashmir. When you take the road from Kashmir to Jammu, halfway through you make an abrupt left and it leads you to this valley where the very air is charged with supernatural sensations. Kishtwar is in the hands of its women, whose regal gait and conversation style reveal their status. People say that the beauty of Kashmiri women is well known in all the nations that surround us. But we in Kashmir talk about the women of Kishtwar. We say they are beautiful, but beauty has nothing to do with it. The truth is that we are in wonder of these women because they can cast spells, which no one can remove.

Roxanna's story is a chilling one.

She says, "My great-grandfather's friend went to his posting without his family because it took months to travel in those days. So his wife and small children stayed back in Srinagar. He lived in a small forest hut in Kishtwar and a village woman came to do the chores for him. At first he did not notice her but one day he saw that she was amazingly beautiful. She seemed to become more perfect as the days passed and he fell in love with her. The woman came to live with him. He could think of nothing else but her, and forgot all about his family. He did not go home, even for a visit. His wife suspected that he had come under the spell of a Kishtwari woman, so she went to a holy man who gave her an amulet that she wore. The amulet worked, and the man, suddenly seized by nightmares and illness, was awakened from his stupor. He decided to go home for a visit. At home with his wife and his children and his parents, the man recovered from his insomnia and his seizures. Caught up in the delights and comforts of family life, caressed by the ministrations of his devoted wife, he forgot about the woman in Kishtwar to whom he had promised he would return within a month. He asked for and was given a transfer back to the head office, on medical grounds."

Roxanna has us in the palm of her hand. She says, "One morning as he was getting out of bed he looked outside his window and saw a bird of the most unreal plumage sitting on a tree branch staring at him. Its shining feathers caught the sunlight and blinded him with joy, and he staggered and sank back into bed. When he tried to stand up again, the man seemed to have lost all power in his legs. The bird sat on the branch, with its head slightly inclined. Its fixed gaze tied the man's sight in a knot and he could not look away or close his eyes. He was unable to sleep, or sit or eat or stand up on his feet. Day after day he lay in bed wasting away as he looked out of the window. His family tried all manner of remedies, physical and spiritual, but the man seemed to be paralyzed. When the family followed his vapid eyes they could not see the menace staring at him through the window. They just saw an ordinary bird sitting on a tree, and even though it seemed to be there all the time, they thought nothing of it. In a few weeks the man was reduced to skin and bones. Then he passed away, still looking out at the bird, like a shell out of which everything had been sucked. The moment the man died the bird flew away."

"Witches," says Roxanna about the women of Kishtwar without any condemnation in her voice. Most of the people in her family are in the forest department and they know that little valley well. "Their eyes are green and blue from the emeralds and sapphires in their mountains. They make magical events happen. If they want something you can be sure they will get it."

It's strange, but I don't ever remember men talking about the witches of Kishtwar, it was almost as if talking about it made them vulnerable.

"How can you tell if a woman is a witch?" one of us asks.

"Look at her feet, if they're backwards, she's a witch."

We are reassured; we know how to find them out and save ourselves.

"Remember, if she wants to she can fool you into seeing her feet as normal." That hurls us back into the realm of uncertainty and fear.

"What do they do?"

"They have annual contests at which they throw a live snake into the sky," she says. "When it comes down they ask someone to cut its belly open. There is nothing inside. It is as though everything has disappeared."

We have heard similar stories of these magical women at home. There is a sense of relief that Kishtwar is a day and a half from Srinagar. A smaller valley, accessible only by perpendicular snakelike mountain roads.

"What about the men?" I ask.

"Oh, the men cook, and knit at home or play the flute or beat their drums as they sit by the fields that their women plough."

I remember a Kishtwari ex-cook of ours who is a baker's assistant now but knits sweaters for extra cash and comes over to our house sometimes looking for work. He always challenges us to catch him knitting a stitch, and we never can. His hands move so fast that we think he is pretending to knit, but a patterned panel appears steadily from below the frenetic hand movements he makes with the needles and the wool. We enjoy his visits because he always brings us freshly baked roghani nan stuffed with ground lamb.

If you know how to bake bread you can always find a job in Kashmir. The demand is constant and increases every day. Our native breads, of which there are many varieties, are all yeast breads baked in an oven. The baker is as essential an everyday vendor in Kashmir as the milkman and the greengrocer. We start our day with freshly baked loaves. In all of India this is peculiar only to Kashmir. People like to say that because we eat sesame bagels and wear skullcaps we must be the descendants of one of the lost tribes of Israel, but I think it may have something to do with the fact that we are deeply influenced by Central Asian culture.

We have a tradition of baked yeast breads of different varieties for different occasions. Housewives must always have breads and rolls on hand. My particular favorite is roghani bread, round and flat, a pattern on the top dragged by the baker's fingers, coated with poppy seeds and seasoned with fennel seed, salt, and butter. Some villages are famous only for their special breads and we often go ourselves or send someone for miles to fetch these specialities. Bakers symbolize more than the staff of life to us. They have a special place in our minds, because it is said that one of our mystic ladies jumped into a baker's oven and ascended from its purifying fires to heaven.

But bread is nothing without tea and we drink tea all day. Our samovar, more Oriental and ornate than the Russians', has flavored sweet green tea perpetually on the boil. The minute a guest enters our house and sits down, tea and bread are proffered, no questions asked. When a girl gets married in Kashmir, breads in all their versions are ordered in quantities for the days of the wedding when we have a house brimming with relatives who will be drinking sweet or salt tea and eating appropriate breads as often as they are offered.

Weddings must be held in the summer. It just makes more sense, provided auspicious dates are available on our calendar. It is getting time for me and girls my age to be married and our families are on the prowl looking for prospective spouses for us. They have to start early, whether Hindu or Muslim, or when the time comes upon us it might be too late. Our mothers are building up a hoard of the usual trousseau items, the best of everything that comes to the house, but being superstitious they are circumspect about it. Every year that the trousseau lies in storage the pressure increases to find the right boy. My mother is obsessed with the fear that either I or my shawls, or my gold or silver, might in some unanticipated way become tarnished and thus unfit for a wedding. She wants to have my wedding arranged and done while everything is in immaculate condition, but for one reason or another things keep getting delayed.

My mother's quest for a son-in-law remains unfulfilled even after a couple of years. Her pleasure and anticipation in collecting my trousseau is turning into a headache of responsibility and tension.

It is time for my horoscope to be consulted again, since things are not working out. No suitable young man has materialized, and the ones who do show up have unacceptable drawbacks. Armed with the horoscope that was written for me at birth by our family priest she sets out to consult a master of the occult with the same seriousness with which one looks for a doctor for a sick person.

The writing over the entire length of the scroll is in geometric black *sharda* script and the auguries and planetary configurations are punctuated by vegetable dye paintings. Designs of docile-looking women with indocile bosoms and behinds, and sloe-eyed men, and animals that strongly resemble humankind border the astrological charts. Our priest is an astrologer and an artist.

Having unfurled yards of the prophetic document drawn up at my birth, the astrologer looks at it intently, turning it this way and that because planetary charts have to be seen from all angles. He rubs yet another unshaven chin—shaving daily is not at a premium here in Kashmir. The astrologer slurps his tea in the noisy fashion so acceptable to all of us, sucking in the tea with a vacuuming noise from the khos he holds with a hand towel. He swallows the hot tea in a big gulp and then comes up for air. It is a sign that the tea is quite delicious.

I say to myself, "Storm in a teacup. This is where they must have got that expression." The nuns have taught us how to be ladies and take tea in little sips.

The astrologer draws a sharp breath, then he looks about him, as if scared of looking at my horoscope, at which point my mother looks decidedly crestfallen. The astrologer waits as if debating whether he should deliver his verdict, and then, assuming a doctorly expression, he tells my mother evenly, "Your daughter is like a choice piece of meat surrounded by wolves."

He is right, of course, about the general ambience of my situation.

Then he says to her, "He will live like Rama and look like Krishna."

My mother nods with relief at this oblique reference to a son-in-law. No Shiva for me but two incarnations of Vishnu rolled into one man. This is completely acceptable. At this point anything is acceptable.

But my resemblance to select mutton has sent my mother into a complete panic and doubling of search efforts for a proper groom. She has already gone past the first list, has considered the second tier, and is now looking at the third tier of eligible boys. A girl must be married off, maybe not to the best possible choice, but even a not-so-good-match is a hundred times better than an unmarried girl. Trunks of my trousseau are gathering cobwebs in the attic, vying for space with the pickles and seasonal vegetables, tomatoes, eggplants, squashes, all dehydrating in necklaces, pushing the house spirit to the edge of his limits. The attic is a hub for preparations for futures of all kinds, and perhaps this is why it provides ideal lodgings for the house spirit. But it is getting a little cramped now.

The delay in my marriage weighs heavily on my mother's mind. She looks worried all the time now. College is fine, but in her eyes it is just another feather in my marriage cap, a guarantee of normalcy. Only girls with serious disabilities do not go to college, because education is free in government schools and colleges.

I don't really remember what my college education means to her. I am quite sure it is a necessary rite of passage in her quest to get me "settled." Perhaps I feel the same way. It is not very clear at this point.

My mother was married at the proper age of fourteen to her father's best friend's son, with whom she had played as a child. She went from her mother's home straight to the sanctuary of her in-laws, who lived two houses away, even though it might have seemed a strange and unforgiving place to her. She grew up in her husband's home.

Before she was married my mother left home only for special occasions, there was no question of socializing with her friends in a public place or even going for shopping sprees on a regular basis. When she did leave home she was accompanied by her mother or a dependable senior servant. She received her education at home; tutors put her through all her grades until she took the school certification examination given by the university. She had no plans to work, no one expected her to, mainly because she did not need to. She got married, had children, and became completely embroiled in her domestic world.

My mother wants the same safety net for me. She knows I will want to work, and that is fine with her as long as I am part of her world. But she is beginning to lose sleep at the thought that if she does not tie me up to a man soon I may lose my moorings altogether and be lost in space, where you never know where you are or where you are going. She wants to be able to identify with any predicament I may find myself in, so that she can protect me. She is terrified that I may take a path where she cannot find her way to me. When I become a mother all these things are revealed to me, but back then I find my mother's emotions and concerns stifling and outdated.

My dim matrimonial prospects may be depressing, but they do not discourage my mother. Being a mother she does not give up hope, and she repeats to me, as her mother repeated to her, "You belong to someone else, you are the property of another household, you have been entrusted to me by God, but I am just your caretaker. May the Almighty bring that day upon us soon when you go to your own home."

If this were not standard conversation between all mothers and daughters I might have suffered completely irreversible psychological damage. But all of us have heard this so often that it does not traumatize us. Or perhaps we believe in it ourselves to some extent.

"May God have mercy on you and send you your husband soon," says my mother. Then she comforts herself by saying, "When the time comes, it will happen so quickly that we might not have time to prepare for a full-scale wedding."

For many years she cheers herself up with these forward-looking upbeat statements, but ends up having insomnia for two years before I find my cosmic half. But she is right about something; it happens so quickly that she does not have time to plan for a full-scale wedding. I cannot imagine what having more time would have entailed, though. Through the years her trousseau shopping has continued apace and a sizable portion of my father's earnings is by now wrapped up in cotton- and silk-embroidered tablecloths covered with bitter flowers and locked inside steel trunks in the attic.

Not everything is sent upstairs. Some items, no matter how desirable, never make the trip up to the attic. One year merchants of indeterminate origin from an obscure little town in central India arrive at our gate on bicycles carrying a large collection of antique Kashmir tapestries. No one has woven these *jamavars* for over a hundred and fifty years and none can make them any longer; contemporary revival efforts look like caricatures of the originals. Kashmiri weavers perished when the shawls were mercilessly if accurately copied by the thousands on machines by Europeans. After the ruination of the Kashmiri craftsmen there was a tumble of regimes, and somewhere in all these changes the art was lost forever. No one has been able to successfully weave a true jamavar since.

There is some hesitation and debate about the antique tapestries among the women in my house, but after persuasive sales talk by the chief merchant they agree to give him a chance to open up his merchandise. The men are shown into the drawing room; it is quite different with our indigenous shawl man who goes straight into the inner rooms. When the jamavar merchant spreads out his shawls on a white damask tablecloth there is a musty cellar-like odor about the shawls, confirming their antiquity.

With his eyes and voice lowered, the antiques merchant puts on a bit of a dance, a bit of theater, to carry on the theme of royal court procedures. He wants to lend authenticity to the provenance of his tapestries, which could in fact have only been owned by royalty and nobility. But the poor man is at the wrong place. Far from being flattered by his courtliness, the ladies in my house are perturbed and sit on the farthest sofas as if afraid of contamination.

My mother makes her pronouncement.

"The shawls were used as shrouds by maharajahs, or given to the priest to appease the gods in case of illness, or to combat the evil eye, or pay for sins committed by royalty. We don't want any of these things in this house," declares my mother to the astonished merchant.

No one dare challenge this forbidding decision, which is totally lacking any documentary or even circumstantial evidence, because my mother has always been counted on to do and say the right thing. We are averse to anything secondhand or worn by anyone else, as if that person's karma rubs onto his used clothes. And, of course, for a bride everything has to be fresh and virginal and, like the bride, previously unowned.

The merchant's assistants flash us contemptuous looks, muttering the unutterable under their breath as they leave.

The youngest of the lot straggles behind and says impudently, "Why don't you buy a plastic Taj Mahal?"

That does it for my mother. The Taj Mahal is a tomb of the heart and any mention of such a place at a time when she is looking for untainted trousseau gems is not to be tolerated. Fortunately by this time the antique dealers have safely entered the neighbors' gate.

Mother collects my trousseau like one possessed, because that is the way it is. She has her mother breathing over her shoulder. My maternal grandmother disapproves if my mother even indulges in a cup of tea at a restaurant, saying, "That money could be put to better use by the mother of a marriageable daughter."

My father, modern son of a modern father, has succumbed to the obsession as well. The business of marriage is so critical that most parents live very plain lives and save in order to ensure a proper wedding for their children, both boys and girls. This is not an option; this is something that must be done. For the parents of a girl the process starts at childhood because shawls and jewelry are involved, and it continues until the girl gets married and leaves with her dowry.

It seems so ridiculous that I, an educated working girl, should still bring with me wool fabric and gold as security for rough times at my husband's hands, but it's an old habit. We do not give up venerated habits that easily, not unless we are forced under pain of death.

The summer continues to produce other vendors bringing goods from faraway places. But it is the tourists rushing to escape the heat and dust–winds of India and clamoring to buy its superbly crafted wares that Kashmir waits for single-mindedly. Tourists are a brief but lucrative annual phenomenon and put a whole year's bread on the table of most Kashmiris. We ready ourselves for them in the winter when no farming is possible and we have to stay indoors. We keep ourselves occupied through the lengthy winter by fashioning handicrafts, sewing, painting, weaving, embroidering, and carving.

When the tourist season arrives our shops are stocked full with the wood, silk, wool, and leather handicrafts the visitors buy so voraciously. Even so, anxious merchants, remembering cold wintry nights, employ every trick to sell. All is fair when it comes to outsiders. The boatmen do up the red and yellow window awnings on their boats and houseboats. Buses are freshly painted, with flowers and blunt phrases such as "Arrive in peace not in pieces," and other lessons learned on hazardous mountainous roads. The tourists buy everything and engage every hotel and mode of transportation.

Summer is a festival in Kashmir.

The busiest shopping area is the Bund, a promenade on the river Jhelum a few minutes away from our house. The lanes leading up to the Bund are lined by silk and leather merchants, taxidermists, bespoke tailors, jewelers, silversmiths, restaurants, shawl merchants, banks, and English-style bakeries.

The shawl peddler's sons also open up a shop near the Bund and in a collective venture of all their ancestral trades sell highly prized silks, carpets, and shawls. My grandfather's tailors also move their shop from the seventh bridge down in the old city to the new shopping area, carrying with them his measurements and those of my ancestors, and now ours as well. We existed on their frazzled ledgers, caught at a moment, the height and length and breadth of the last four generations of us, and now we are carefully re-sewn and bound in new leather.

※※※

The tourists vanish at the end of the season and in the valley it's just us again, no outsiders, no strange languages. Just us.

"You have to be very careful when you leave the valley," says my patriotic grandmother. "There are all kinds of people out there."

We have always been here, we are born here, we grow up, study, get married, work, and die here. In our minds the best place in the world is Mother Kashmir, which is what we call home. Everyone knows everyone because we have the same mother. We do not want to be anywhere else, particularly in the summer, which we have enjoyed in our way for generations.

Our world is quite complete, nothing is missing. We have our routines that we enjoy tremendously, ordinary as they might be. The postman comes around five in the evening and sits down on the porch steps. He waits for my grandfather to read the mail, after which he is given an update on family news; he considers himself entitled to the information and we agree. After all, he *has* seen everyone grow up before his very eyes. The postman, the vendors, all are Muslims, but we hardly notice that as it makes no difference to us.

The fishmonger, the milk vendor, and the greengrocer, arrive with predictability every day at a likely hour; they come up to the round verandah where they usually find someone. Preliminary greetings are followed by oaths swearing the high quality of their wares, though the milk vendor has not been able to persuade anyone for the last forty years that he does not amplify his milk with tap water. We tell him that we are skeptical, but every year he is the one sent to the new homes of our married daughters on their husbands' birthdays. Then he goes carrying large wide-mouthed terra-cotta pots of creamy yogurt covered with blanched almonds, saffron and silver paper, a birthday gift that tastes excellent while ensuring longevity.

Friends and relatives arrive at our porch, frequently and often unexpectedly. We don't expect advance notice, and we never know exactly who might show up. We accept them with their foibles, just as we do our gods; we have grown up keeping our space intact even in a crowded room. In a joint family system, this is an absolute requirement. One learns not to be dislodged from one's center by another person's proximity, but this is no guarantee against disagreements or heated confrontations. But once it is all worked out we resume our joint family life as if it were the most natural thing to do. Our family stories provide the glue that keeps us together in a stable network.

A widowed cousin of my grandfather's brings us smelts in green plum sauce when she visits us for a month each summer.

This is her claim to fame, her best dish, and a favorite of my grandfather's since he and his cousin were children together. When she shows up at our gate we make a big fuss over her and she makes embarrassed gestures but loves it. A child widow, she is awkward and shy all her life.

When relatives show up we never ask how long they are going to stay. It could be a day, a week, or a month, but we always feel sad when they leave. We walk them to the main gate, stopping to cut some flowers from the walkway as a parting gift, remembering some last-minute gossip. Mostly the conversation is about marriage, those in the offing, those in the past, those celebrated and those regretted, instructive tales that all of us take to heart, although we know that in front of karma there is little one can do about the outcome of a union. Every family has an ugly secret or two, and these are exchanged in whispers, close to the ears. Then glances are exchanged, lips pursed, and heads shaken with disbelief and the matter is quickly put away.

Our relatives from the crowded ancient city covet the abundant flowers of our suburban gardens. They take bouquets of them home, only to tear them up and throw them at the idols in their temples the next morning. Gods like petals more than entire flowers. We are always careful not to smell the flowers intended for the temple. If you smell a flower, what is left for the gods? We always make sure that the garden gate is latched after our visitors have left. This prevents itinerant cows from stopping in to make lunch of our shrubbery.

The real inspiration for our small gardens lies beyond the city and beyond compare: Shalimar, once the field of jackals, and Harwan, still a forest of birds, and all the other Mughal Gardens set around the Dal Lake like gems in a necklace. In one of the gardens, near one of the terraced fountains, is a plaque inscribed by a Moghul emperor in the seventeenth century, "If there is Paradise on earth, it is this, it is this, it is this!" We know how he felt. Should there be a wedding in the wings and the couple require a romantic push in the right direction we know just the place and the time. A moonlight picnic at Chashma Shahi (where my friend and I called on Pandit Nehru) usually does the trick.

As we climb the hundreds of steps to the springs we can smell the summer grass on the night air. Behind the springs is Pari Mahal, the ruins of the astronomical observatory of Dara Shikoh, the mystic son of the Mughal emperor Shah Jehan of Taj Mahal fame, the grandson of Akbar the Great. Like their founder Dara Shikoh, the ruins are haunted by ethereal beings. At night, if one is lucky, one can see these elusive creatures flying around in a playground from which they cannot escape.

We travel to the Mughal Gardens in tangas fully equipped with lunch, carpets, and musical instruments. After a ride on the boulevard surrounding the lake we disembark, and the garden we choose depends on the mood or the occasion. Then we spread out our carpets, and put a samovar full of green tea on the boil.

Today we are at Nishat Bagh. I see an old friend of my grandparents playing the sitar to a tabla accompaniment. Satkak is a very tall, slender man, perhaps elongated would be a better description, because he looks like a Kashmir poplar tree. Thin wrists emerge out of his loose caftan sleeves, and on one of his long fingers he wears the *mizrab* with which he plucks the sitar. His eyes are smoky blue and he is a devotee of musical soirees. At weddings when the musicians sing and dance on the henna night he is so moved by the lyrics and the melody that he leaps to his knees from the carpet on which he sits and then stands up in rapture. He throws out his long arms to the performers and the heavens, loudly offering to sacrifice himself to the fates in lieu of the musician-dancer who has brought him to his feet.

The dancer is always male, in female garb, and we all applaud when he makes a rose out of the corner of his pink veil and thus concludes his song "Where have you blossomed from, my lovely rose?"

Satkak is with us on the picnic as always and we try to make music with him the best way we know how. He plays the sitar, someone plays the tabla or a seated piano accordion; someone else plays the *tumbakhnari,* our one-sided hand drum, only seen in Kashmir. It is a terra-cotta vessel with one opening covered by real parchment leather, we hold it in our lap, and we learn to play it as children, on smaller versions. Most of us are adept at this popular instrument. Less accomplished members of the family play improvised folk accompaniments of two brass khos working as cymbals or an earthen cooking pot and a bunch of keys. The even less musically inclined heat lunch on top of a kerosene stove and serve it to the rest of us. Or they may blow hard down the samovar funnel until the chinar coals are red-hot enough to bring the sweet green kahwa tea to a boil.

As we picnic at any one of the Mughal Gardens we have a view of the lake in front. In the distance we can see the outline of Akbar the Great's fort at the Hari Parbat hill, which is also the ancient residence of one of our most powerful goddesses. The symbols of spiritual and physical protection are in full view as we eat and laugh. We will need both in the years to come.

But for now we are engrossed in the business of summer, walking in the formal gardens among the arbor vitae, cedars, cypresses, and water fountains also bequeathed to us by the emperors, and maintained tenderly for centuries by the gardeners of Kashmir. We return home at sunset.

҂҂҂

Some summers we travel to the Mughal Gardens via the lakes in a houseboat that we rent from a grand old Muslim lady, whom we call Rice Blind. The entire household packs up for a week-long trip on a waterway that takes us through canals, locks, and lakes, ending at the Mughal Gardens. Rice Blind was in-troduced to us when Tulli came to my grandfather's house as a bride. She is practically one of us and has participated in our household activities all her life. Now she comes to spend a day with Tulli and to help us clean our rice after it is hulled, to sepa-rate the chaff from the grain. They talk all the time, sometimes in whispers. The lady cannot see very well, but this does not re-sult in her being kept from a task for which even people with good eyesight sometimes find themselves ill-equipped. She has what it takes, instinct and intuition; both are more powerful than mere eyesight. Our rice is perfectly cleaned, and according to one of our more poetic cooks, blossoms like a lotus when prepared.

Rice Blind used to be a milk-mother in the old days, but now she chaperones those very daughters when they get married. She is prosperous and owns several houseboats, but loves to accom-pany us on our trips. Her sons are the boatmen. We simply love her as she holds out her arms in an embrace, clasps us to her and offers herself to the fates in exchange for any evil that might be-fall us. We believe sincerely that fate accepts substitutes.

Summer celebrations are the same for Hindus and Muslims. After hibernating in the long winter we seize the other seasons and stay outdoors and in the sun as long as we can, enjoying our supernaturally exquisite valley. We have everything in com-mon—our food, our music, our language, and humor, our Sufi tradition and shrines, our blossoming fruit trees, our lakes, and rivers, talking endlessly over our common fences. Other things we do differently, although nothing comes to mind immedi-ately, except the following of our separate faiths.

Most of all it is the water that seems to provide the common backdrop for all our lives. Our ethos is drenched in water, in-formed no doubt by the plentitude of deep, wide lakes and beautiful rivers in Kashmir. Superstitions about these waters and their produce are everywhere; we treat our waters with caution.

The waters, though, are far from pure and in some parts near the city quite polluted by human waste. But we do not take the water for granted. Spiritual pollution causes grievous fear and trepidation among Kashmiris. Even as late as the nineteenth century we did not dream of sporting with our water, and only put it to serious and unavoidable use. But a Scottish missionary discovers us, falls in love, stays and eventually manages to persuade his Kashmiri schoolboys to participate in boating races and regattas. The logo for Tyndale Biscoe's school even today is two narrow crew-style crossed oars, but it was a hard-won triumph for him.

Sometimes Rice Blind's sons pull up and anchor the barge poles, and the arklike boat, which is built like a long one-storied house, comes to rest. The boat is furnished with reed mats, and the wooden floors are seasoned with use to a smooth polished shine. My grandfather and his sons go for a leisurely swim in the river, while their still-Eastern women pray inside for their safe return. Mr. Biscoe has not managed to convince everyone in the valley: having a bath is a must, but swimming for pleasure might upset water spirits who are always lurking beneath among the swaying weeds and the lotus roots, happy to ensnare and drag down disrespectful Kashmiris. The men leap back on board after a daring swim, and cheerfully if sheepishly pull out the beer that has been surreptitiously traveling the lakes with us. The lake water is cold enough to chill the beer bottles that hang in a net hooked to the boat side. The women love their green tea, but smile knowingly at a couple of the others who linger suspiciously over a metal tumbler.

Sometimes we pass a wedding party in a houseboat and participate transiently in their convivial world of incense, music, and dance. Our wedding incense is a handful of seed that we throw on live coals, a Persian habit with a Persian name. We use

isbandh to dispel the evil eye or evil spirits, and to create a cele-
bratory ambience. The smoke and perfume and sound given
off when it sputters and burns on red hot coals is a quintessen-
tial part of wedding nostalgia. Mesmerized by the sounds and
smells, we stare after the joyful boat long after it has become a
speck on the horizon where the lake meets the mountain. We go
back to playing cards or singing and wait for our meals.

What meals we enjoy on the boat! Fish are caught, fried, and
quickly polished off. The hot sun and the cold beer, the fried
fish, the river and all of us on a boat—it is a rare combination of
time and place.

We eat off round wide lotus leaves twice the size of dinner
plates. I am loath to call them "disposable," but that is exactly
what they are. I can still remember a large drop of water rolling
around brilliantly, like mercury, on the velvety emerald-green
leaf. Rice Blind's stalwart sons move the boat along with barge
poles as we drag our hands in the water, clutching and pulling
out the lotus leaves as the houseboat glides through the dark,
bottle-green, weed-filled lake.

The process of catching fish provides the greatest excitement
for us children, and the adults are no less enthused at the prospect of fresh catch cooked right on the spot. Kashmiris eat river
fish, lake fish, and brook trout from the mountains. But being a
people obsessed with water we have an enigmatic relationship
with fish. I have seen both my grandmothers cook fish with care,
anxious that the inviting aroma of frying fish might attract
some unforeseen calamity. On the other hand, we serve fish at
dinner prior to a traveler's departure, certain that the lingering
fishy smell will see him safely to his destination.

Some fish are forbidden to us. We would rather die than
touch or even hunger for fish from sacrosanct springs, the residence of mythical snakes. Ours is an honored timeless under-
standing. The springs are clear green, mysterious, and strangely
peaceful, tucked away among the mountains.

Given our preoccupation with fish it is no wonder that Fatha the fishwife is a great favorite at our house, a regular fixture every week. In spring, summer and fall, the fishwife, accompanied by her son, makes the rounds of our neighborhood, opening gates and crying out boastfully "The best, the sweetest, most unique fish in the world!"

We call them in, mother and child, and the fishwife comes through the garden gate carrying the fish kettle on her head. She sets it down on the granite path leading up to the porch where we choose the fish we want. After a great amount of haggling, laughing, and mock anger, the deal is struck. Then she weighs the fish before taking it around to the garden hose in the back of the house where she will clean it for us. Her little son follows her.

Fatha guts, scales, and cleans the fish at the garden faucet in the backyard. With expert hands she and later her son take a sharp knife to the soft white underbelly of the fish and effortlessly slit it open pulling out the contrasting bloody red entrails. Within minutes the offal is disposed of, the fish washed under the hose and sent into the house in wicker baskets still dripping water.

The fish are sent in to the kitchen whole and then cut into pieces by the kitchen staff who will prepare them for us. We have some favorite fish dishes: my great-aunt's smelts, and fish with tamarind and kohlrabi or daikon radish, and best of all fish cooked with fresh lotus root, as if to provide the fish with familiar surroundings in the hereafter.

One of the first kitchen tasks given to my mother as a brand-new daughter-in-law was to help cut the freshly cleaned fish into steaks. She had hardly been inside her mother's kitchen, being somewhat spoiled as a first child. But eager to please she gladly took the basket. She lifted the basket cover and passed out at the sight of six pairs of fish eyes looking up at her. In spite of this debacle she learned to cook the finest fish dishes for her family. The story is added to others on the family sampler like the motifs on an ivory silk archive, and we hear them all repeated again and again.

I participate in and identify with everything that happens at my home and have to thank my grandfather Shyamji, for pointing out the theater in our everyday existence. He is my best friend and companion. When I return from college he puts down whatever he is reading and wants to know exactly what happened between the time I left home and my return. I considered it a privilege to share my day with him, not once do I regard it as an intrusion. For his sake I keep my ear out for faux pas and other delicious news items, and relish the thought of the expression on his face when I repeat them all, accentuating and embellishing along the way to make the story worth hearing. When the weather is right we have chairs taken out on the small lawn in front of the house, and if the weather is inclement we sit on the porch. I particularly love sitting on the wicker chairs on the lawn, which is hedged with evergreen bushes and flowers.

Sometimes we read or gossip, sometimes he corrects examination papers in silence. But there must always be tea. Tea is nothing grand, just Kashmiri hard rolls or bagels, or samosa, or buttered toast with jam sometimes, and the tea itself, which is either green kahwa tea or Darjeeling. My grandfather's university colleagues and friends often join us on the porch, or in the garden. When they were younger they played tennis together; now they go for walks, and laugh and talk. Sometimes they play serious bridge.

I loved that welcoming porch with its round balcony and rotund white pillars. A picture of the porch hangs in my office now. When I look up from my office desk here I can see my grandfather sitting on his favorite chair in the porch corner, with his hookah pipe or cigarette in one hand, book in the other, waiting for me to come back from school, then college, and then university.

One day when I come back from university I find one of the

farmer's sons from our rice fields sitting on the porch with my grandfather. We are out of donkey season now so I ask my grandfather why he has come. The donkey caravan has dwindled to just three or four animals now, the farmers own the land they till, but the farmers are still like family. My grandfather looks a little mystified.

"I don't know," he says in English to me, "but this fellow is telling me a cock and bull story about some strangers turning up at their village at night. He says they are very tall and broad, and wear strange hats, and they might have weapons. They have taken rooms in the village. They buy these people's clothes and want to look like Kashmiris. They want to learn Kashmiri. I don't know what he is talking about."

In a Kashmir village a stranger used to stand out like an unfamiliar tree.

Grandpa looks fondly at the boy, he treats him like a son.

We are so used to our village folks bringing us stories of witches and wizards they have encountered in the fields at night that we think this is just a modern twist on the theme.

"Really?" I say, looking curiously at the farmer's son.

"He says his father sent him to let us know but we are to do nothing about it. He looks quite frightened if you ask me. I wonder if his father knows he is here," says my grandfather. He indicates to me that the farmer's son is a little simple-minded.

We reassure the young man, Mohammedu makes him some tea, and we give him some bus money and send him back. We never hear anything about it for some time, but we are dead wrong about the farmer's son. "Infiltrators" have been sent by Pakistan to foment an uprising among the Muslims in the valley. But they find no collaborators, even though they are backed up by Pakistani-owned American Sabre jets flying thunderously low over the valley. The eventual deconstruction of the valley has begun, but we cannot believe it or don't want to believe it. So, the visit of young Ali from the rice fields is put away, mixed with other events, like bitter flowers scattered amid the comfort and warmth of what we prefer to believe.

We go back to enjoying the summer of 1965. The green grass under our feet is a seasonal gift, one has to make the most of it. We walk barefoot on our dew-soaked lawn before sunrise, getting our feet wet; it is the best thing for your eyes. We spread a woolen rug on the grass and take a nap there in the afternoon sometimes. A high wooden wall marked by square brick columns gives us the privacy we need in our front garden. We can hear people talk as they come and go in the small lane outside our home, but they can't see us. As a result we overhear some very interesting conversations, particularly when smitten boys and girls of the two segregated colleges just around the corner from our house use our lane as a detour on their way home. Our lane is an ideal trysting spot, although the college lovers keep a shy and requisite distance from each other, sometimes walking on opposite sides of the lane. Inevitably the lane acquires the unofficial name of Lover's Lane. Everyone clucks disapprovingly, but only a fanatically prudish relative actually chases after the students waving my grandfather's umbrella. No one can enjoy life if she is to have her way.

My grandfather is relieved to get his umbrella back.

"Careful," he says. "These days the young people come after you, and then you are in trouble." He is half joking because he does not like moral policing, but at the time he has no idea how prophetic his words are going to be.

Tea on the summer lawn, the camps and the hikes, the gardens, the lovers' rendezvous, are over all too soon. In a few weeks autumn starts, with a leaf here and there, and then all the chinars burst into flame red and then the leaves dry into brown before falling to the ground. I love to drag my feet and shuffle through the crisp chinar leaves as we go for our evening walks. We have to start earlier each day as it gets darker and colder. Whirls of smoke from little fires made from the fallen dry sticks and leaves of the chinar surround us. The weather and the colors are mellow, and it suits me. The fruits are ripe, taken from the trees, the fragrance of ripe apples is everywhere, and the mountains will always be there.

As the weather turns colder still we reluctantly withdraw and spend more time inside, until it is winter and we come indoors. Then the room stoves are lit and all the doors and windows are shut for the season, except for airing every morning. This is usually done before we come down, and by the time we awake the rooms have been cleaned and aired and the stoves started.

Every winter my grandfather's friend and next-door neighbor Tathaji sends him a message in an envelope in the hands of his housekeeper. When my grandfather opens it he finds a bit of melting snow, it is an announcement of the first snowfall. This means that his friend saw the snow first and surprised my grandfather, who now has to treat him to dinner. This is an old tradition, but my grandfather always forgets to beat his friend to the game. The surprise is clothed differently each time, and every year we have our neighbor over for a meal. Of course, it is just an excuse to liven up things in winter. Fortunately, they only have a fence between them.

When the snow has fallen fast and furious and the sky clears, leaving a yard or so of soft snow in the ground, my grandfather and I set out on a favorite adventure. We love to make the first footprints in the snow in our lane wearing our high black rubber boots. He wears a Burberry bought for him in England half a century before by his brother and I am wearing an overcoat of Kashmiri tweed woven at our local mills. I have a feeling that along with paisley and cashmere the Scottish tweeds have Kashmiri ancestors as well.

When my grandmother was young she said the snow fell to the height of a man. When I was growing up it fell to the height of a child. Now the trees are gone from the mountain forests, cut down greedily, the reports from Kashmir say, and the trees have taken most of the snow with them. They tell me that in Kashmir now they are lucky if they get a few inches of snow.

My grandfather was not a wealthy man, but he lived a rich life. He taught English first at the men's and then at the women's college. So almost the entire college-educated population of Kashmiris passed through his hands, because everyone took English whether they were arts or science students. We could not board a plane or bus or attend theater, enter an office or a shop, or even go for a walk without someone coming up to greet him. He wanted to know everything about them, and unabashedly enjoyed the benefits of having fond ex-students in all the right places.

After Shyamji retired, he and his band of colleagues, veterans of the professorial establishment, continued to see each other frequently. They discussed politics, academia, literature, and their own beloved Kashmiri culture and history, which has deep roots in Persia. He, like his ancestors, was well versed in Persian and taught me how to read the future from a volume of Diwana-e-Hafiz, an anthology of Persian verse by the Sufi poet Hafiz, by invoking the poet's beloved Shakh-e-Nabad. I remember that when I sought my *faal,* or future, the verse read something about empty wine cups and deserted wine houses and my grandfather said it's all superstition anyway. I was not so sure.

One day, when my grandfather had retired long enough to start getting on my grandmother's nerves, the doorbell rang. Some somber-looking bearded men in Persian-style turbans and caftans and pashmina shawls, pillars of the Muslim community, were standing on the verandah looking for him. Shyamji met them in the drawing room and then came out once to ask for some tea, which we sent with the male servant on a tray in a special Japanese bone china tea service.

After an hour or so my grandfather saw the men off at the gate. When he came back to us in the family sitting room he had a delighted look on his face. He told my grandmother that no longer was she going to have to worry about him lounging about because he was going back to work. The men, most of whom were on the board of a new college, had just invited him to teach his subject, English, at a new college based on Islamic precepts. They requested him to teach there because they wanted nothing but the best for the college that they had started. They also asked him to invite other colleagues eminent in other subjects, now retired as well, to join the faculty of the Islamic college.

My grandfather was honored and gratified that these distinguished old men had come all the way from the inner city to look for good teachers wherever they could find them. He was so proud of his valley, and genuinely believed, as did the rest of us, that Kashmiris were blessed with an extra gene for intelligence.

This was wonderful news indeed. Not only would Shyamji continue to receive his pension, he would now also get a salary that was double what he got in his time; pay scales had risen with the cost-of-living index. So, one would find him humming as he went for a walk or puttered about the house or garden. As a young man he gave up teaching his first subjects, Chemistry and Physics, and went back to university to study English Literature because it had become his passion. What could be better than being among students and books and in a classroom? Retirement did not sit well with him. The anticipation of renewed contact with his poets, essayists, and novelists rejuvenated him quite perceptibly. He accepted the offer and started teaching right away. When he left for college every day he was as enthusiastic and dapper and well turned out as always.

Things continued like this for a few months. Then one day he returned almost immediately from the college. Something was terribly wrong, I could tell, because he never looked unhappy unless some great personal loss had occurred. We did not say anything as he hung up his coat and trousers in his wardrobe and changed into his leisure clothes.

I brought him a cup of tea on the porch and he said, "I have handed in my resignation."

We could not believe it, it was not something he nor anyone else ever did back then.

"Why?" I asked him.

"The students only want Muslim professors. They threatened us Hindu staff members with dire consequences if we did not resign immediately." I had never heard him disheartened before.

The college board, mostly learned men of the old school, was embarrassed and dismayed. They apologized, but they said they could not do anything in the face of such overwhelming popular opinion among the student body.

"This is the new crop," they said. "We don't know who planted these seeds."

My grandfather looked as though he had been hit with a blow from behind.

We could not make any sense of it; this sort of a divide had never surfaced before. My grandfather was sure the students would see the error of their ways, after all, they were like his own sons, but that was not to be. We resumed our daily life, he waiting for my porch stories, sipping tea with visiting friends both Hindu and Muslim, or riding his bike all over town, and my grandmother a little more charitable now. Shortly thereafter the police chasing a mob down our lover's lane woke us up one night.

There was a protest on the main road, a road named for the British Resident in pre-independence times, and that was broken up by the police. Some young men fled into the safety of our lane and were hotly pursued by the police on foot wielding batons. The protesters ran out at the other end of the street demanding something, but we could not quite make out what they were shouting at the top of their lungs. There was a palpable sense of physical harm and fear for the first time in our neighborhood as the night resounded with slogans.

Someone from our house crept up to the gate and peeked out

slowly and came back to tell us, "They are demanding freedom and Pakistan, they are shouting anti-India slogans."

We were used to sporadic expressions of anti-government sentiment, but it had never happened right under our nose, and had certainly not been serious enough to cause anyone to get beaten up by the police. The separatists had dared to express themselves in public in our neighborhood, only yards away from the residence of the Chief Minister of our state and the government machinery. If we had paid attention we would have realized that the anti-Indian voices had gathered a movement. Perhaps we knew, but it was unthinkable and we left the realization unexpressed, hoping that the truth would go away.

Mohammedu said, "They don't want to study, they want to be arrested and have their exams postponed. That is what they really want. If they had to work hard and stay away from their wives and children to send money home they would realize what a sacrifice an uneducated man has to make to feed his family. They would just get back to their books and make something of their miserable lives, earn their bread." But he looked perplexed and not very sure about his assessment of the situation.

We were all uneasy, despite Mohammedu's on-the-spot analysis. We could never have imagined that one day these young men would be prepared to make the ultimate sacrifice for their beliefs and that these sparks would set fire to the whole valley. As we turned in for the night it was comforting to put the whole occurrence down to the craziness of restless young men with nothing better to do.

The next morning I woke up and went out to the balcony outside my bedroom on the first floor. Our house was called "The Poplars" from the time a curtain of those tall slender trees stood alongside its garden wall and the garden had fruit trees. Then the river Jhelum overflowed and Srinagar was flooded once again. When the floodwaters receded they took all but one each of the poplars, cherry, apple, and fig trees as booty.

The round balcony was directly above the porch and over-looked the neighborhood. I looked down and saw the fig tree just inside the garden gate, gnarled and old, sedate, with ripe, soft purple figs, sweet red flesh inside, ready for the picking. That morning for the first time I noticed how vulnerable all the houses were. They looked like a collection of fragile homes, rather than a genteel enclosure of friends who had lived together quietly for the better part of a century. It felt as though the *paridaeza* had evaporated, leaving us in an ordinary neighborhood, open to intrusion and chaos and change.

Although our homes were made of bricks and stone, our doors and tall windows had plenty of glass. It did not occur to us that a single stone could gain entry into the interior. Beauty had been more important than fortification. The houses had plenty of woodwork, and wooden balconies and ladders and staircases, wooden floors. Even our ceilings had three-dimensional hand-carved wooden parquet called *khutumbandh* or "no beginning no end," a work of art and artfulness. In short there was wood everywhere.

A single match in our humidity-free dry environment could have reduced the houses to rubble. The thought was new and chilling. No one insured their house or anything of the sort, but we had started to think differently now. I am not sure that there was even an insurance policy one could buy that would rebuild a house. We felt somewhat disoriented, but in the calm that ensued in the following weeks we willingly forgot that evening of discontent.

The calm did not last for very long. Ugly rumors of unheard of things happening in the old city reached us, and everywhere an unsettling number of police personnel were in evidence. No one talked about it openly, but the air was alive with uneasiness. Amazingly we continued with our lives, playing ostrich and refusing to acknowledge that in the heart of the valley events were moving in contradictory directions. I can only attribute our attitude to the fact that what we were going to lose was so rare and profound that we preferred to believe the impossible.

Our family, ever ready to seize life, ever ready to disregard any discordance, went up to the mountains in the summer as per usual, We camped in tents, went horseback riding and trekking into still higher mountains until we hit glaciers or the snow line. We bathed in icy rivers, went fly-fishing for trout, and thoroughly enjoyed "exploring the outdoors," as my grandfather was fond of saying.

On one such occasion I had the distinct feeling that someone was looking at us from the pine forests on the mountains across the river, just opposite our camp. When I informed my family over lunch they said, "Mad little girl"—an appellation that had stuck with me well into my college years—"what a fertile imagination."

When we returned home to the city, we read in the newspapers that we had camped just a few minutes away from a bricks-and-mortar camp for guerilla trainees. The anti-Indian political movement had broadened and spread underground, political protest had multiplied, and no one seemed to know what to do about it.

We did not see the fishwife for some time and had to buy fish from a fishmonger near our local temple. Then one day Fatha appeared again, a shadow of her former self, emaciated and haunted. She informed us that the police had arrested her son and accused him of terrible things. The police tried to straighten him out by "ironing his political difficulties" with a hot pressing iron before releasing him from custody. He had barely survived and required constant medical attention that she could not afford.

She was a widow now, and she still had five small children at home to feed so she had to get back to work. She looked in fear for her life. She said, "The old city is full of foreigners who do not speak Kashmiri. We cannot see them; they only reveal themselves to our boys, like angels of doom. Our boys follow them blindly, I don't know what honey sticks to their devilish hands. Many sons in my neighborhood are missing. Some have returned home as mujahideen, some have turned up dead, and some have completely disappeared."

The cry for independence had become a holy war. Holding her head in her hands Fatha looked down and wept. "I don't understand any of it. Wonderful young boys are finished. The mothers and fathers have gone mad and are running up and down their street screaming for their children to return."

I could hardly bear to think of what had happened to Fatha's son. I had seen him grow up from a small shy boy who peered at us from behind his mother as he clung to her pheran, to later helping her with her fish business, to finally selling fish for her. He had asked me to take his photograph once and I had agreed. He pulled out a cap and a pen from his waistcoat and, having combed his hair and arranged the skullcap on his head and the pen in his pocket, gave me the go-ahead. I had the picture developed and enlarged and presented it to him. His mother blessed me via all the shrines, saints, and the God she knew.

Fatha went back to work as soon as the boy was able to move around on his own, because she had several mouths to feed at home. The boy could not have been fifteen, and for his widowed mother he was everything, but the child she knew had been swallowed by an opening under his feet, like another young boy sent by an old magician to look for a magical lamp.

⁂

Relatives from the old city bring us up to date on the events there, and these incidents seem to be much more radical than what we, Hindus and Muslims in the suburbs, experience. We are mostly government employees or upper-middle-class people with a lot to lose in any disturbance. Today a relative who makes a living as a plumber has come posthaste from the old city. A sickly man, he is pale at the best of times but today his forehead is glistening with beads of perspiration. The last time we saw him was when the water froze in the pipes of the outside walls of our added-on bathroom, and he had stopped in on his way to work.

Shyamji and I watched as Amarnath wove straw around the length of the pipe and then set fire to it, thawing the ice into free flow. Then our relative looked very much the expert as he brought in his tool bag from his bicycle rack. He was wearing a tweed coat and an embroidered maroon wool scarf smartly wrapped around his neck. Amarnath had his eight o'clock meal at our house that day to save time. Steaming rice, greens, and some lamb cooked in turmeric and yogurt, standard sunrise breakfast for office-goers, that lasted them until dinner, except perhaps for tea and a bagel at the office. Amarnath was a hard-working and ingenuous plumber and would have done well if it had not been for the fact that his lungs were weak and he would fall ill very often. The only reason he did not get fired in spite of his absences was that he was a dependable government employee.

Today Amarnath looks disjointed; his eyes are vague.

He says, "Some Muslim men have been arrested because they found a young Hindu boy in the lane next to ours with his stomach slit open and his guts pulled out. The poor fellow was returning home from college and his books lay scattered all over the street. There was enough blood to color drains for several neighborhoods." Amarnath stops to pull out a handkerchief and wipe his face. "This is the beginning of a terrible time for us. What are we, just a few homes surrounded by thousands of Muslims? We could be mowed down in one night. It could be any one of us next."

He is a grown man but he wipes his tears like a child, with his palms, and I think he is not only crying for the young man but for the tragedy and loss that has struck us all in the valley. We cannot bear it that such hatred has replaced complete trust in our intermingled lives. He has never cared to count how many pandits lived in the city, there had been no reason to do so. He lives simply, and struggles like his Muslim neighbors to make ends meet, but like them he is mostly content with his lot. Serfdom for centuries had built a strong bond of commiseration and common cause among us Kashmiris. Now the bond is not a sure thing, everything he has taken for granted is threatened, and he is no longer free but in fear of his life, the future of his family. He has nowhere to go, he cannot afford to move anywhere, nor does he want to go anywhere. This is all he has known; he lives in the house that has come down to him from his great-grandparents, in a *mohalla,* a neighborhood where generations of their family have always lived, going back for millennia. He has never thought of himself as the representative of any country. He is just a hardworking man, like his neighbors with whom he has shared his woes through the years. It is not possible for him to think differently. His neighbors now think he should go to India because he is a Hindu, but India is an alien place for him just as it is for them, and only Kashmir is home.

We give our cousin a cup of tea and bread but a definite pall has descended upon us, and this time we cannot wish it away. In the past when things go awry we go to Hindu and Muslim soothsayers, but no amulet can reverse this situation. All of us, Lotus Eaters and inhabitants of bewitched gardens, have to wake up and come down to earth. We must put our feet on the ground if we want to stand up and survive. It is dark, and there is no moonlight, our days and nights of revelry are over for the foreseeable future. We cannot lie in wait secretly for fairies anymore, worldly omens are closing in on us.

The dead boy's soft pale stomach had been cut and gutted just like a fish, with a sharp short knife, the kind you use for fish. Fatha found her son's knife and bloody clothes under one of the wicker baskets in which she washed her fish and screamed out hysterically, bringing in her neighbors, both Hindu and Muslim. A scuffle ensued and when the police came in they took her son away again. Her head hung on her chest as though her neck was broken; she had sent her angry son to hell. The fishwife-mother's whole world lay about her feet, drenched in blood. If only she had known better, she could have protected him; if only she knew what bitterness he had grown into. But he had entered a merciless world and she did not know where it was and how to get there.

No one could remember anything so bloody in the heart of the old city, where everyone lived so close together that no one could even have gardens of any consequence. Hardly anyone could bear to talk about it. Nevertheless an us and a them was evolving and growing, and the rift between us Kashmiris, the Hindus and the Muslims, was widening like a chasm in an earthquake. We could not see it, though, and when we met our old friends and neighbors it still felt as though we were all on solid ground. Perhaps we preferred to believe that there was no breach underneath us into which we could fall in a moment of foolishness.

The self-determination that had been promised to Kashmiris by Nehru can no longer be swept under the carpet. It has become a war cry and a weapon of destruction for forces beyond anyone's control. Rebellion is spreading like a slow, sure fire even though we ignore the smoke that is everywhere about us.

The Kashmiris are divided into those who want Pakistan to win Kashmir in a battle with India, those who want an independent Kashmir, and those who want the status quo. Kashmiri pandits naturally do not want the Islamic state of Pakistan, but then neither do some Muslims. In any case, as less than three percent of the population, it really does not matter to anyone in India or Pakistan or Kashmir what we pandits want, and we will pay with our very existence for that. Our history has taken a terrible turn through no fault of ours.

Every day brings more demonstrations and arrests. We are not carefree anymore, we cannot mix freely, or talk freely, and suspicion colors everything. On the surface people go about their business, maintaining a semblance of normalcy. My friends as always are mainly Muslim and the composition of our group reflects that of the valley, one or two Hindus for twenty Muslims.

We still enjoy being together, it's a habit since the beginning of time, but for the first time we treat each other warily. We do not discuss politics at all, and we are careful, we want to avoid any friction. As we tell each other, "God forbid I should have to choose between you and my child if there is a riot, I would naturally choose my child, as you would." This conversation only takes place among close friends, among the others it is tacitly understood. We Hindus are living a foolish dream that all is well or going to be well. To any one of us who cares to see with their true eyes, we are now an endangered species, destined for a scattering from our homeland and eventual obliteration from the face of the earth.

The trouble is that like the Muslims we pandits call only the Valley of Kashmir home; Jammu, which is a part of our state of Jammu and Kashmir, does not qualify. If we cannot carry our mountains, our lakes, and our fish with us, we don't want to go.

We are becoming increasingly despondent. All of a sudden we feel we are far too few, far too outnumbered, and far too vulnerable. Our lives and dignity have become imperiled in our own homeland. The Indian government is the sworn enemy of the mujahideen primarily because India is a Hindu country. Being Hindus we are suspect in the eyes of the rebels, who are now calling the shots literally and figuratively in Kashmir. The mujahideen only want Muslims in the valley.

We used to live and die in Kashmir, the thought of going elsewhere did not arise. People from everywhere clamored to buy property here, but only Kashmiris, born and bred, were allowed to do so. Now no one wants to come here out of love for the valley, and many of us want to leave, each for our own different reasons, but most of all for the fear, distrust, and hate that corrodes us even as we breathe.

I entered my teenage years and college at the same time, and now as I am turning twenty I sit for my master's examination in Political Science, a rebel against the family vocation of English Literature. The final examination for my master's degree is accomplished in bits and pieces because the political disturbances bring an unending stream of curfews upon us. We rather welcome the delays initially because we are really never fully prepared for the examinations, which require us to memorize everything and then spit it out on the answer book. So every day extra is most welcome, but after a while even that becomes tiresome and soon we are chomping at the bit.

Eventually we manage to take all our examinations. My friends and I finish college and university with flying colors, but this makes no difference to our mothers. In their eyes, prior to marriage we are just waiting for our real home and it is getting really late for us. My accomplishments do not impress my mother, she thinks I take it all too seriously and is rather embarrassed by my resilient bachelor status. We don't make a fuss about it but the fact is that we are eagerly looking forward to becoming working women. Things have changed since our teenage years. We want to get married and are quite excited about it but having a career has become very important. The nuns and the women's college succeeded in making women out of us. Normally we would have looked for jobs in the valley, but the political turmoil does not augur well for anyone's future, and it looks particularly dismal for Kashmiri pandits.

There are mothers and there are mothers. My mother cannot sleep at night because of an unwed girl and an overcrowded attic. The fishwife mother flails about at night, and she stays awake during the day as well so she can feed her other children. There is no tangible devil she can kick out of her miserable existence. Mother Kashmir watches her children draw blood and degrade the valley with betrayal and putrefaction. We have lost our innocence, and there is a lot to hide from each other now. We are engulfed by an incomprehensible darkness, and we grope in the eclipse, looking for answers.

Daughters

I would not have left Kashmir in the summer for anything, but I have been appointed lecturer at a women's college in New Delhi and this is my first serious job. I am happy to follow others into the family profession. My plane takes off from an airport surrounded by mountains, leaving in its wake fields of wildly swaying red poppies. I exchange brilliant Kashmir skies for the wilting, dust-laden heat of the plains.

In New Delhi's summer one quickly gets into the habit of bathing three times a day. It is the only way to survive, to cool down and wash away the perspiration from temperatures of a hundred and ten degrees and more. Living through the added catastrophe of one hundred percent humidity, though, is impossible, and when things go beyond that inconceivable limit I just resign myself to a corpselike existence, unable to do anything in the unfamiliar oppressive season. I will eventually get somewhat used to it, but in the beginning it feels as though I have died and gone to hell. This is a long way from summer at home.

We do not have expensive air conditioning in Delhi, but use a contraption made of a screen of cooling *khus* grass, which is liberally doused with water to create moist air that is then fanned into a closed room. It is an ancient device, now electrified. The room with the cooler smells and feels like a dank stable but is still preferable to the alternative available outdoors. The heat slaps you down, and if you are not careful you may never get up. Summer in New Delhi is a nightmare.

It is quite clear now why we had nothing but sympathy for Kashmiris who had to live outside the valley and endure unbearable weather. Through the centuries Kashmiri pandits have undergone several diasporas to other parts of India because of intolerant foreign Muslim rulers. Once again Kashmiri pandits are in an upheaval, some running to safety, some digging in their heels, some still trying to figure out if things have really gone beyond the imaginable. The question that runs around in my mind is, Where do we go from here? We have fled persecution many times before, but this is the first time we have been set upon by fellow Kashmiris.

During one of these upheavals several generations ago, a family of Kashmiri pandits who lived by a canal in the valley left for the plains of India. One of their descendants nourished the Indian freedom movement in its early stages, his son carried the movement to success and this son's daughter is now the Prime Minister of India. Naturally, we, like the rest of the world, are fascinated by Indira Gandhi. She symbolizes an unlimited professional world for Indian women, and for Kashmiri women in particular.

I have thoroughly enjoyed the profession of my grandfather Shyamji, teaching. Having grown up with the rhythm of college life, class discussions, and books, teaching at the college had come quite easily to me, as it had for many in our family. But my grandfather was a learned man, and I fancied myself to be more a person of action than of books. Besides, I saw a Kashmiri pandit woman running India and it seemed to me that I had no choice but to give it a try as well. Thus I decided to give up teaching and sit for a competitive civil service examination. After the results are announced it is pointed out to me that I have become the first Kashmiri woman to be selected to the Indian

Administrative Service. The news is greeted with skepticism by my parents; I seem to have taken another step toward open unconnected space, out of their enclosure. They do not know what this could lead to, but I have made up my mind to join the service.

After selection we undergo training at the Administrative Academy, which is located in the Mussoorie hills. The heights of Mussoorie seem to be the right place for us to embark on training courses and a career that will take us on a smooth ride to the top levels in government. We also have a wonderfully disproportionate situation at the Academy, six women and a hundred men, all just out of university. We are young, in our twenties, euphoric at being the only ones to pass a civil service examination in which there were forty thousand candidates. After the nuns and the women's college, the constant presence of a hundred-odd young males in and after classes is exhilarating. It is easy to work and to play at the Academy, and this is an exceptional time in my life. I seem to be moving in all the right directions.

The clouds and pine forests of Mussoorie also make a welcome change after the soupy heat of New Delhi. Though these hills cannot compare with the striking heights of my Kashmir mountains, they have a certain romantic look. The mist floats in and out of the winding roads that cut through the deodar trees and there is a familiar and delicious chill in the air. Mussoorie is a place created entirely for British families escaping the deathly heat of India. Some empire builders died here anyway, from other assorted Indian perils. Elaborate headstones in the Mussoorie graveyards record young and old would-be maharajahs that never made the return journey home.

Kashmir is a different story. It is not a *hill station,* as the British called Indian summer resorts, for the simple reason that we have mountain ranges rather than hills. We regard even good-size hills with nonchalance because our mountain ranges are the tallest in the world. This is not our only claim to fame. The ancients, Persians and Greeks among them, wrote about us, we have two-thousand-year-old ruins of a university from a time when Kashmir was an academic mecca for Buddhists and Hindus. Then we were a major watering hole for traders on the Silk Route. We have also been a vast empire. We are not a creation of any of the many foreign rulers whom we have seen come and go. We Kashmiris have always been there and we know it.

※※※

I go back to Kashmir for my summer leave. It is wonderful to be back, but within a couple of days of my arrival there is a disturbance in the old city. A curfew is imposed but everyone is quite used to it and works around it. We rely on our stored grains and garden vegetables, the ubiquitous eggplants, tomatoes, greens, and kohlrabi that everyone grows. All we have to do is scatter the seeds and irrigate the soil, which keeps its end of the bargain. There are no pesticides or fertilizers, and the vegetables are unparalleled. We still use agricultural methods made popular in Mesopotamia, even though the telecommunications age has dawned on us and the telephone exchange is right around the corner from our house.

※※※

My training is over soon after I return to Mussoorie. It is time to face rural India, which is my real workplace. I have been posted to an ancient city, Allahabad, where three rivers meet, the Ganges, the Jamuna, and the third invisible but ever-present, Saraswati. It is just a day and night's journey by train from the academy but a far cry from its colonial world of dressage and paddocks, personal valets, and formal dinners.

Allahabad, the birthplace of Nehru and Indira Gandhi, is

also the hometown of one of my colleagues at the Academy, and he is present at the train station to receive me. By sheer coincidence he is also a Kashmiri, but his family left the valley several generations ago in one of the many pandit diasporas. He does not speak our language but nevertheless considers himself a full-blooded Kashmiri. I am to be a houseguest with his father until I find my own accommodations. I have come south of Kashmir halfway across India and my friend will go the other half south to Madras to his posting, very far from his home. It is gratifying to find at least one familiar face in this strange new place.

If I had wanted a job that entailed being active I certainly got more than I wished for. My job description is impossible, because it encompasses everything. I am part of a bureaucracy that is basically unchanged from the time of the last Mughal emperor who owned everyone and consequently was in charge of everything. It is a vast anachronistic machinery, a British hand-me-down, ragged finery spread like a net that is holding back a nation bursting with the desire and energy to move forward into a new age.

The British bequeathed to us free Indians a legacy of British-style courts and codes of law. But we have quickly shackled ourselves again with corruption, mismanagement, and poverty. Nevertheless, like my colleagues in the Indian Administrative Service, I must go through the motions and do what little I can.

The four o'clock tea at the Academy with petits fours and bite-size cucumber sandwiches brought to our rooms, the riding instructor, formal mess dinners, all are a distant memory. Now I look forward to *katchery* tea, which is named after the courts, and the same open-air stalls supply boiling tea and native snacks to the magistrates and the lawyers, the accusing and the accused. And there are crowds of us. After the rarefied atmosphere of the Academy the flies are somewhat disturbing, but I don't mind because the snacks have just come out of cauldrons of boiling oil and they are hot, spicy, and delicious.

The district is a world apart from Mussoorie, which is a world apart from Kashmir.

The difference must have been the same for the British officers whose footsteps we are following, but when they went out into the field it was not their country. The 370-odd villages under my jurisdiction are the villages of my land. I cannot leave the court at the courthouse, and lie awake at night thinking of a young daughter-beggar who shows up at her mother's hearings in an illicit liquor case. Her mother is accused of running a roadside brewery behind a storefront of hot tea and chickpea snacks. Now the store is gone and the daughter tells me that after court she heads out to the streets, to beg she says, so she can pay the lawyers. The staff in the courtrooms are no strangers to these refreshment stalls.

The range of humanity covered by this job is unbelievable. At one level I rub shoulders with the heads of government, and at the other end my duties take me to a netherworld of criminals. I supervise eagerly corrupt junior staff, militarily clean police stations. I am surrounded by urine-stained jails, the malodor of living human beings and dead ones, petitioners with leprosy or blindness wearing mud and bloodstained clothes because they have no other change of clothing. In the middle of the night I am woken up to be rushed to take dying declarations from lips sputtering blood and words. Some corrupt magistrates take even the vegetables painstakingly grown for their own consumption by the inmates of the jails they visit. The inmates watch magistrates come and go with contempt and alienation and go back to a lunch of dry flat breads roasted in the open.

Prostitutes dance in the compound outside the district court, giggling and flirting with the seemingly unconcerned policemen who lead them to court for "affray" and other misbehavior because they cannot really prove prostitution without the male being present. The policemen sit down under a tree to rest as they puff at a lowly whole tobacco-leaf *bidi,* which they share with their arrestees. The serious offenders are manacled, or in leg irons. I will never forget two hot-blooded young men, twins, about twenty, caught in a revenge killing, sentenced to death. They had beautiful heads of hair, and were full of life. As I approached the Sessions Court where I was training they asked the mobs to make way for me. Then they moved back in chivalrous fashion as I took my place in court. The court compound looks like a grotesque carnival that comes to life the minute the courts open for business. At night, when justice is not being meted out and the halls of law are closed, all is peaceful.

At the other end of the spectrum I am invited to the Governor's Palace where I enjoy chilled lychee juice served in a silver glass. I am an appointee of the President of India and hold office at his pleasure, and can only be removed at his command. It is all quite heady, but our perspective is quickly restored when we go back to work in the field. There is a night-and-day difference between life at the seat of authority and the world that depends upon it for justice.

In a general atmosphere of colonial drowsiness where nothing moves except for flies, I attempt the impossible. The fact that I close cases with files half a yard high after decades of court impotency is almost revolutionary. A friendly lawyer tells me that I cleared a tunnel in case files that date back to pre-independence times. It is clear to me that if I was looking for swift action quickly leading to palpable results, I am in the wrong place. There is no difference between night and day, this is a twenty-four-hour job. There is hardly any difference between right and wrong, and I have little to show at the end of the day. I will be running as fast as I can, and I will still be in the same place.

The case files have been festering in storerooms; they are brownish yellow and frayed at the edges, and they smell rotten. Evidence presented to me in every case seems awfully similar as I note it down. It also sounds very familiar. I recognize the deadpan language of the prosecutor when the witnesses speak in his clichéd colloquialisms. But I say nothing. I give him the benefit of the doubt. I say to myself that he has a noble end for which he has employed unforgivable means. I am an unwilling accomplice in throwing a basic principle of jurisprudence out on its ear, assisting him as he plods through his underpaid and thankless job. Add to which he has the vilest-looking pimples that were ever witnessed on a man, and these are hardly mitigated by his ingratiating smile.

The witnesses look as familiar as the language they use in court, the same sheep to the slaughter every time, although they are judicially presented after appropriate absences. Quite obviously the witnesses are well-coached professionals and exist on a roster of some kind from which they are rotated for court appearances. They are cooked either way, and they do not have a choice. If they give evidence against their kind they are outcasts in the slums from which they come. If they don't comply with the police request for evidence there is no slum that can hide them.

This is the city hall aspect of my job. The fact that I am a woman causes no impediment. If anything, people seem to be sure that justice will certainly be tempered by mercy when I attend to their problems. I hear evidence and write judgments on gambling, law and order cases, as well as some civil cases. I am an administrative officer, so serious criminal and civil cases are sent to the judiciary. We have not evolved much since the resident magistrate was a Britisher holding up his bit of the empire in this dusty old town.

Not unlike the Britisher, after the sweltering heat of summer I look forward to the relief of the monsoons. The most acceptable part of the year in the plains for me is the winter when the weather remotely resembles what I am used to in Kashmir. This is also the time when I camp out in my villages for a month.

We arrive at the chosen village and set up camp on the village

green as it has been done for centuries. This is the first half of
the tour, and covers half the area under my jurisdiction. Living
quarters are prepared for me in a large tent while my retinue settles into smaller tents. The difference between us must be maintained; we have the ghosts of winters past all about us. We go
through the motions of making sure that map and field coincide
and the owners have not been dispossessed, although the names
on the records mean nothing to me, a city dweller. The village
clerk has held his post for decades and knows who is who and the
exact location of their land, but he is not saying anything and
for the sake of sanity I prefer to have implicit faith in him. I am
yet another neophyte magistrate sent to this posting and soon I
shall be on my way. He is the real permanent civil servant, the
only sure thing in the fluctuating politics of a democracy. But he
is not as unbiased as he should be, because his palms are slippery
with excess grease, an entrenched perquisite of his job.

Villagers crowd around the encampment, where a makeshift
office is set up every morning. I take petitions from the villagers
and listen to their woes. A war widow screams that the land that
has been measured and given to her on paper will be snatched
from her at night when I have gone back to the security of my
camp. She stands in front of me, the official in charge, but her
eyes are turned toward the lowest-level village functionary who
holds her in thrall, as he does the whole village. I can almost hear
Gilbert and Sullivan in the back of my head as I announce to
the village that I shall rid them of their grievances and attend to
their needs.

I do the best I can under the circumstances. My staff realizes
that I can make a nuisance of myself if they get up to any real
mischief and my watchfulness keeps them somewhat in line. In
the end, though, I have to rely on them to execute the orders.
They know and I know that my tour of duty is short, and soon
they will be free of me when I leave their inaccessible village and
return to the city. My winter tour lasts only for the mandatory

twenty-one days set aside by the British. Next year it will be another magistrate in training.

After work I sit outside my tent on a chair set in front of a desk inherited from a long-dead British magistrate and wait for tea. It has been a long day, starting just before sunrise, but as the evening settles on the ripening fields around the camp, it is peaceful and soothing. I remember our summer camps in Pahalgam where the view outside our tent was that of the Kolohoi glacier and other snowcapped peaks. This is beautiful, but entirely different.

My attendant, enduringly called a *peon* from the time of lofty British overlords, brings me a tray with tea in a large mug from a ceramic factory under my jurisdiction. Some hot snacks, boiled potatoes garnished with lemon juice, fresh coriander, green chilies, and tender peas made the same way are on the menu.

I keep a careful account of the expenses; it is not right to expect the villagers to support the encampment as they used to do in our feudal and then colonial past. No, this is emancipated India, no slaves or serfs or subjects; money must be paid for services rendered by high and low.

My accompanying staff, who have been at the office for almost my entire life, are old hands at this game. They humor me with a painstaking account of the eggs I eat, or tea and sugar, and I pay every night after accounts, but I seriously doubt that the villagers who supply the stuff are going to see any of the money. In fact, what I pay for my food is probably laughable compared to what the villagers pay my staff to make sure that their land records are in order, or to bring some problem to my attention.

I dutifully ask for the bill. The peon ritualistically, as if in vaudeville, reads out in courtly fashion the items consumed and the costs incurred. Behind the singsong style of account rendering I detect a certain fun being had at my expense. It would not surprise me that the camp cooks are behind my tent watching the shadow of the peon on the gas-lit tent canvas as he, one hand in the small of his back, the other hand holding out the sheet of paper, head at an angle, reads out the expense account like a proclamation. The cooks are probably rolling around with laughter in the grass outside while the head cook admonishes them with a sly smile on his face. When we all retire for the night I pull down the flap of my tent and tie up the laces and think about the smell of pine needles and a boisterous river at a camp in a distant valley.

Music from my transistor radio eventually helps me sleep on the hard bed I have requisitioned from the house of the village chief. Perhaps it is because of the tents and the camp atmosphere, but I fly to Kashmir for the night. I see Rice Blind wearing a chintz pheran and a soft white muslin scarf on her head. All is not well. She holds out her arms to me, and in her palms is newly hulled rice, and she looks at the speckled grains and says, "This is not Kashmiri rice anymore. Just look at this. What are these strange grains mixed in with our rice? Can you see the dust and blood? Everything is unclean. I can do nothing."

Rice Blind has tears in her eyes as she clasps me to her bosom, and I can smell the sun in her cotton pheran. I wish I could tell her that I also realize this is not the Kashmir we knew anymore. There are so many strangers in the villages now that no one even lifts up their head to stare at them any more.

The mujahideen, well provided by foreign reinforcements, are positioned to fight the troops and they terrorize soldiers and civilians alike. Rice Blind's eyes are the azure skies of Kashmir and white clouds float across them as they tell me that the real thing is ever more elusive in Kashmir. I cry with her, in the dream I know is a dream. We are both helpless in spite of our heartache.

I wake up next morning to a beautiful winter day, almost as warm as a summer day in Kashmir. The weather is too good to sit inside and my staff sets up a breakfast table for me on the grassy patch outside the tent. Like my grandfather I am indoors only when I have to be. I look around at the yellow mustard flowers in the green fields, and it is a clear soft day, but I have a distinct sense of unease inside and cannot get Rice Blind out of my mind. Where is she, how is she? I pull my chair closer to the table and wait for breakfast. When will I go home again?

My breakfast arrives. A courier from the city has brought me my newspapers. Things are getting worse in Kashmir, if that is possible. The contents of the newspaper sit in the pit of my stomach. I don't want breakfast.

My peon, Siraj, reminds me that I have not eaten. I look at the breakfast tray and see a small dish of yogurt. The cream is so heavy on top it defies all laws. Where are those laughing gypsy women from the mountains, with their faces framed in a thousand minute braids, who brought us buttery yogurt in terracotta jars as they had been doing forever, and their forebears before them? The newspaper says that Muslim women in Kashmir have been sent back in time and are required to wear a burqa that covers them from top to toe. Disobedience brings archaic punishment from the moral police who are mostly women. My friends and contemporaries threw off the burqa first at the college gates and then at home, but the daughters of these liberated women cannot leave home now without the total veil.

What is going on in Srinagar? What do people eat? Do they still go for walks and boat rides? I know these are ridiculous questions, but I ask my family in my letters. One reply tells me that professors at the colleges have to tread carefully when teaching literature, or political science. Discussions on Truth, Beauty, and all we "need to know" are met with a stony silence from the nervous students. It is better, they say, to stick to hard facts and to stay away from philosophical subjects.

I seek refuge in my all-consuming official duties. At the end of the day when I have waded through a sea of humanity and have driven home on roads riddled with potholes, my insides thoroughly rearranged, I am too tired to think. But I have a job to do and I want to do it well. So I take the peon's experienced advice and eat something before I start the day. Who knows how far into the interior I have to go and when I shall return?

For the second half of the winter tour we stay at a dak bungalow. Thank goodness for a brick building with the added luxury of a verandah and a view of the village in the distance. The bungalow is a postal relay stop; it used to be a resting place for the ever-itinerant and watchful colonialists. A new batch of village records, connected problems, and assorted villagers all have to be inspected. At day's end I return to the bungalow. On the verandah a few wicker chairs arranged socially in a circle wait for occupants. I sit down on one and listen to the silence as the evening becomes night. There is no electricity and a primitive darkness grows around us by the hour; the only light is from a handful of stars scattered like seeds across the dark blue sky. Surrounded by unoccupied chairs I look out into the distance. The outlines of the ruins of a mosque are faintly discernible. I ask my Muslim peon about it as he hurries toward the verandah with a gaslight in his hand.

"Oh," he says, "that is a dead mosque. No one prays there because it is haunted by djinns. No one lives long after praying there and the last person to pray there died along with the exiled Mughal emperor in Burma." Siraj knows these parts like the back of his hand, having accompanied magistrates every winter for decades.

The British fastened onto Indian soil after killing the princes and deporting the last Moghul emperor who languished and died in an alien prison. The British never read his poems mourning his murdered children and his lost homeland, and his imminent death on foreign soil. We Indians sing these songs even today, and somehow it does not seem so out of date. The tragedy of dying in unknown territory speaks to everyone.

Everyone wants to go home at the end of the day. Even djinns need to return home and the mosque next door seems to suit them just fine. But the genies next door are bad djinns.

Siraj explains, "They eat the hearts of people who pray there, that is how they live and how the people die."

Not a comforting thought, but mortals in my beautiful valley have committed monstrosities far more deadly than what mere djinns might muster. We have outdone the very demons we sought to keep at bay.

I must admit, though, that for all the unseen and seen challenges I face in my job, I have very comfortable accommodations, attentive staff, and security. My police counterpart is also present with his entourage, but he keeps an appropriate distance. He needs my magisterial powers to order police action, and I the magistrate have no arms or legs without him. It was an ingenuous way for the Raj to keep two Englishmen out there among the natives out of trouble.

Still, I would give anything to look out at mountains. In the horizon where the great heart of a historic nation meets the sky in a flat straight line, I feel the absence of mountains deeply; I look out and there is no undulating line of familiar jagged peaks, no snow line. As night falls, the staff melts away into the barracks at the back of the camp, and I enter my room with a heavy heart. This is no existence for a person used to being surrounded by a large family and perpetual friends. Kashmir is too far away.

The gaslight exaggerates shapes and sizes in my room. The

lizards on the wall and ceiling throw dinosaurlike shadows. And try as I might I cannot get used to these creatures whose only gross purpose is to devour insects. In the pursuit of this relentless task a lizard might get carried away and fall off the wall and land on the cement floor with a sickening splat bursting its stomach, spilling its blood and guts everywhere, or worse still, fall right into my plate of rice and lentils.

I hear stories of lizards shredded in the ceiling fan. It is a mercy that I am spared this abomination, although a small bird did once fly into my courtroom as it was in session in a gambling case and let loose a hail of feathers everywhere; nothing was left of the body. It had been a hot, steamy afternoon and everyone was in a state of deathlike monsoon lethargy, just a nod away from being fast asleep. The wasting of the bird woke us up. My vegetarian office attendants, thoroughly revolted as they were, dutifully and in very short order cleared the courtroom of feathers and bits of bloody flesh. I think we all pondered the frailty of existence after that interruption. I let off the three young men who were in for gambling by the roadside "in full view of the police station" as the prosecution alleged. The public prosecutor did not even grunt, as he was wont to do when dissatisfied with my judgments. Neither did the office staff harangue the accused for bribes before giving them their acquittal papers.

We do not have ceiling fans in the valley in Kashmir because we don't need them. I tell myself that I will never get used to the heat and the humidity of the plains. Winter preoccupies us in Kashmir. Summer and monsoons define life in the plains.

It is quiet in the village bungalow, and the fixed stares of the lizards on the wall enhance an already sinister ambience. I feel better when my peon brings me my dinner, and some burning incense sticks in a holder for the perfumed smoke to keep little flying bugs away. I can smell sandalwood, rice and chicken curry garnished with fresh coriander, like everything else around me, the real and the surreal, inextricably blended. The vegetables I am served are choice, tender; none is a day older than tastefulness warrants.

I look at my shadowlike attendant with the big kohl-lined eyes. Siraj has a petite frame and is smartly dressed in a black Nehru jacket and white trousers. He is standing at attention just inside the door. Behind him in silhouette in the open doorway is the haunted mosque. Siraj's only job is to be at my service, but he does not stand a chance should even a minor djinn make an appearance. Even so, his presence is comforting as he delicately chews his betel leaf and swallows the red saliva it excites. This is because he is in my presence, otherwise he would have spit out the *katechu* juice. I am cognizant that I am the only woman in the camp, but the office staff is used to it. Like the villagers they have seen women and men officers come and go and nothing impresses them.

After dinner the peon replaces the white light of the gas lamp with the flickering yellow flame of an oil lantern. I lower the wick so that I can fall asleep in its semi-darkness. As I turn in for the night I can hear my mother saying "I hope you realize this is a job for men."

A relative has informed my mother that no man in his right mind would marry a woman with a job like mine. Her insomnia and my career are both in their second year. I believe, like my grandfather, that I can do anything I set my mind to. She believes that I will come to my senses one day and relieve her of the burden of having an overaged unmarried girl on her hands.

I have bolted the door, fully aware that a bolted door means nothing to a djinn. Lying in bed, unable to sleep, I look out the window in my room. Someone has painted the woodwork in the window without even trying to avoid the glass, a typical government contract job. Through the paint-swathed glass pane I see the turrets of the haunted mosque.

Tomorrow I must ask Siraj to fetch my watercolors from the

jeep and set up a table facing the mosque. I can already see my-self painting a light golden wash, letting it dry instantaneously in the warm sun. Then I can define the dome and the turrets of the mosque by painting the sky in glorious cerulean blue, ultra-marine, alizarin crimson, and cadmium yellow. I must finish off the painting in washes of green, crimson, and cadmium yellow to create impressions of the rural grass in the winter sun. I can hardly wait. I laugh quietly to myself and shake my head against the pillow; I tell myself I must get married and live in the post-colonial century and paint and write because that is what I really love. I remain awake. It is difficult to sleep.

I cannot turn up the light and read, the peon on the verandah will wake up, and like him I have to keep up pretenses. These are my villages and they are waiting for my judgments tomorrow. They will carry out my orders to measure and note every inch of land to make sure it is there. If there is a dispute I have to decide it and a certain goddess-like stance is the only thing that will see me through this. I do not have the might of the empire behind me, but I have the wrath and vengeance of the goddess on my side. They are all a little wary of a woman in power, anything could happen.

I think about tomorrow. I have an early rendezvous with the men from the village, who have promised to meet me before the break of dawn in the mango grove. I addressed the villagers at an open-air gathering in the late afternoon, and talked about the benefits of family planning, a euphemism for contraception. At the meeting I handed out condoms, after explaining to the vil-lage that they will not be interfering with the dance, only chang-ing the choreography a little.

As I amplified the joys of birth control the women nodded their heads vigorously, but the men were not convinced. The children's mouths were tugging away at their mothers' breasts, now drained, flattened, and elongated by their prolonged cos-mic role. Then I pointed out how much better it would be if they got rid of the worry of unwanted children altogether through the magic of a tiny incision and a vasectomy. The operation should be nothing to men who battle snakes, and if bitten, perform curettage on their toes with their sickles. These are men who are known to have walked themselves to the hospital with stomachs gored by their brahma bulls. They are hardly the ones to shirk from a little nick administered by a nurse in a clinic.

But I have an impossible task. No child is unwanted to these farmers, and so what I say does not make sense, every little pair of hands is helpful in what can be a pitifully backbreaking existence. Then there is also the problem of trying to have male offspring. The nick does not scare them, it is the idea of changing old habits and provoking nature. They shake their heads to indicate that they are not a whit perturbed, but the women pull their sari ends over their heads to hide their laughter. No one has approached their men with a knife pointed at the groin before and they like the fact that it's a woman who is doing just that.

I say that I shall be happy to take anyone to the clinic for the vasectomy, and of course there is a financial reward as well. The men, women, and children listen keenly to my pitch about contraception, mainly because it is an inescapable prelude to the real attraction, a movie on an outdoor screen. We are capitalizing on the fact that the nearest movie hall is miles away so even a movie on family planning is high entertainment in the villages. After the entire show is over the villagers start to disperse.

Siraj tells me that the villagers will come with me to the vasectomy clinic, but they want to meet me before sunup so that no one from the village sees them go in my van. They will do nothing that might forever cast a doubt on their virility. His statements are like cocoons, a germ of fact wrapped in yards of smooth politeness. It's a tradition that has become second nature to him. It takes me a couple of seconds to decode what he

says, he does not like to call a spade a spade, but the bottom line
is that the men have agreed to a vasectomy. Mission accomplished, I think, as I go back to my small bungalow at night.

I am up at three o'clock in the morning, which is nothing un-
usual in this job. I get dressed, and in the cold dark morning I
proceed with my staff to the mango grove. Through the fog I see
a small group huddled together and marvel at my powers of per-
suasion until the group clambers onto the van. They are the oldest men in the village, horses at pasture, and no one who should
be there is there. But a promise is a promise, and I pack them
into the van and head for the nearest family-planning clinic.

India is ready to burst with new babies. The cosmic dance has
entered a crescendo, and the world is whirling about us. It cannot be stopped, but we are trying to slow it down or the world
will burn out. Shiva's dance is always a prelude to the destruction of the world, but we are not yet ready for rebirth, so we have
to cool his heels.

"But the dance must go on," I can hear my mother say, "or
the world will die."

I spend the rest of the day at the clinic where other colleagues
have also arrived with the villagers from their jurisdiction;
we are overlooking the family-planning project. Doctors and
nurses work in overcrowded operating rooms in record time,
and by evening all the vasectomized men are ready to be herded
into the waiting vans and buses that will take them back to their
villages, their pockets lined with government money. I have no
doubt that despite millions of such operations, nothing can stop
the birth of those who are to come. Still, there is some satisfaction in having tried to stem the tide.

The villagers have no problem that I, a young woman of
twenty-five years, am in charge of the entire enterprise, as are
some women doctors. The villagers see this as a natural phenomenon. On the other hand, to my Western-educated col-

leagues I am a woman-at-large, and in this their attitude is no different from that of my mother, who sees me only as a delayed marriage.

When I return to the dak bungalow the sun is setting in a red sky. I have an early dinner on the verandah. Siraj stands on the grass at a respectable distance, wearing a colonial bearer's red and white sash complete with engraved brass buckle, ready to serve. The jeep driver, a gaunt tall man, with strangely light coloring for this part of India and hair shaven close to his skull, is given to decorating his ears and his jeep dashboard with jasmines. He sits behind the wheel, at the ready, in case I have to be rushed off somewhere to induce law and order, but his sleepy posture is a clear sign that this need will not arise. We are all at our posts, and we mimic the routines of the administrations that have gone before us.

But there are some signs of the late twentieth century. Tomorrow I have to inspect a fisheries project intended to provide employment and nutrition to a village. The money for the eggs and the process of pisciculture has come from an international agency, which has its heart in the right place, but does not have a clue about the village. Neither the villagers nor the lakes want fish. There is great difficulty in breeding the fish, even with the encouragement and application of advanced techniques. Where I come from neither the fish nor the water, nor the humans needed any manipulation in the matter. We did not need to be convinced of the virtues of fish. These villagers cannot abide the smell of fish, the very smell we think is propitious.

What am I doing out here? I would much rather write than encourage fish to spawn or tally land records. This is a world sustained by an antique interwoven mesh of tangible and intangible factors to which I provide only the official seal. I can know some of the truth, and I can dig up some more, but I will never know all within my short tour of duty of a few months, because all is not on paper or spoken. Though this is a challenging and remarkable job, I am not the person for it. I must see to it that I do not spend the rest of my life sitting outside a tent or a dak bungalow eating dinner all by myself with mosque djinns for company. I want to be surrounded by family, friends, and relatives on my porch and good conversation.

Now it is not only my mother who is worried. There must be someone out there I want to marry and who will return the compliment and whom the winds of fate will not blow away for one reason or another. I must get married; I want to have a husband and children and a full household. My parents have not given up, they are still on the lookout, but their demeanor betrays players who are resigned to losing the game.

The winter tour is finally over and I return to my headquarters in the city to discover that I have been posted to the capital city of the state of Uttar Pradesh. Lucknow is an overcrowded, bustling place littered with history and monuments attesting to that fact. It reminds me of a celebrated beauty who has gone to seed. I have an apartment here. The city with its dust and noise is a different story from the fields and the clear morning air of the village. On the other hand here I have electricity, movies, restaurants, indoor plumbing, a social life, and a phone to pursue it with. After a month of biblical vintage village life, these are welcome amenities.

The next week I am on duty with my countrywoman, the Prime Minister of India. I have watched her in admiration through the years from Kashmir, ever since I met her as a college girl. She shares her maiden name with my grandmother; both families had something to do with canals or *nehers,* generations ago. They say Indira Gandhi is more royal than the Queen of England and the only "man" in her all male cabinet of "old women."

I dress carefully when Mrs. Gandhi is in town; she sets high standards and single-handedly revives handwoven saris until they flourish and become wearable art. She has flown in for a public meeting and I am the magistrate on duty keeping the women's enclosures under control. Today she is standing up on a dais surrounded by other politicians and ministers. She does not look like a dutiful daughter now as, lips severely pressed, one eyebrow permanently arched higher than the other, she surveys the scene below her. Like the Mughals, they say, she first feeds the people around her the food she is served just to make sure. This is an easy story to believe; she is the very epitome of power.

A short and chubby pink-cheeked plenipotentiary with red betel-stained lips is dressed in cream-colored silk. He gushes forward toward Mrs. Gandhi, exuding sandalwood perfume, and garlands her with perfect roses. After some time she sits down and he sits next to her and watches her every move like a hypnotized animal. She slowly shreds the roses from the garland and makes a pile of them at her feet, after which she takes her feet out of her sandals and places them on the soft heap of rose petals. The fat man knows that his number is up, he no longer has a square on the chessboard. He has offered her perfect roses, but they are whole. The color drains from his face and this turns out to be one of his last public appearances.

I know why she prefers petals to full flowers.

It is Shivratri, our holiday of holidays, and I go home to be with my family. They are gathered in New Delhi for the winter. Our Shivratri menu has been prepared in full force. But first the prayers to the Divine Twosome of Shiva and Parvati, presided over by my grandparents. After prayers my grandmother hands me sanctified Shivratri food, little roasted rice flat breads with walnuts that have been soaked in water for a week, presumably to remove toxins. Tulli is about to say as she does every year, "For the next Shivratri may you be in your husband's home."

She is about to repeat her blessings, but I stop her in time.

"Don't say that. You know I'll never get married then," I gently reproach her and she does not complete the sentence, but looks thrilled that I have finally tired of being single.

That year I do get married. I think the house spirit, like me, had had enough. I wanted a home and he wanted his lodgings back. There is no other explanation. I was well past the marriageable age, and the befitting husbandly pickings, which were slim to start with, had dwindled to nothing.

I have known my husband since childhood; we are distantly related in a couple of ways, and we have met each other at weddings and other family occasions. The last time we met was at my sister's wedding the previous year, and though our families thought we would make a good match our personal travails kept us apart. This time it seemed we met to get married, and even though we did not say so right away, we were quite open to the possibility. We hardly have been without each other since, because we do very poorly without each other. Ours is not an arranged marriage, but Kishen says he arranged it because he left his job in the United States to come look for me and I am glad for it.

When we start talking it is as though we have been close friends, and we cannot stop talking to each other, almost to the exclusion of every one else. We talk about my work in the rural areas. I tell him some of my adventures and he tells me about his life in the United States and how he decided to go there. He makes conversation in a steady soft tone, unlike me, and his words are measured. My voice goes up and down depending on how I react to something. I am told that I gesticulate and my eyes enlarge when I talk. His eyes tell me that I have his complete attention. I can sense that he does not usually talk this much, but he has a ready laugh and a well-concealed sense of humor. I have never met anyone like him.

We are from the same community and the same town. We are also from the same religion, and being Kashmiris we are from the same caste. This is quite by accident, and was never a priority for either of us. In fact, we both made several unsuccessful attempts to marry people from other communities. It has just turned out this way. When all is said and done, trying to be liberated and modern is no help if your karma is pulling you in the opposite direction.

My husband is good-looking; he speaks well and precisely and always seems to be looking ahead; it looks as though he is wanted somewhere else all the time. He can never fully belong to anything at one time, although he has the reputation in our small community, where no one even dreams of privacy, of being the pillar of his family. He is the product of a vernacular school, excellent in mathematics and science, and has a Ph.D. from M.I.T. If he wants to go somewhere nothing holds him back. He does not have the same umbilical cord attachment to Kashmir that I have.

Even though he is from exactly the same background as I am, he is completely different, and irresistible. I want not only to get married, I want to pull away and out of my present life, where all I seem to be doing is a curatorial job overseeing relics of colonialism. Four years of demented court compounds and somnambulant colonial office buildings have not added up to a complete life. Above all I must escape the interminable summer heat of the plains. I want to have children and make a home, I want to paint and write. I did not want to leave my valley, but now that I have left Srinagar, any place in the world is good enough for me.

With him I could be anywhere.

Our relatives almost shriek with relief when we announce our marriage; they had given up all hope for me. They want to embrace him and take him in, but my husband has lived most of his life alone and, in the United States, likes being left to himself until he is ready to communicate. I think, Thank god we shall live in America—he would not last a minute in my family. They would have felt his earlobes, kissed him, made him eat everything they piled on his plate. They would have rubbed him on the head and ruined his thick hair, which he tames every morning by a combination of pomade and the laborious use of water and a heavy comb. My family does not know what it is like to live nontactile lives or to be small eaters. When I introduced him to my family they were a bit perplexed; he was too formal and bowed slightly at everything and they kept their distance. The look in their eyes told me they were worried for me. But they were quiet on the subject of our differences. I am approaching thirty at an alarming speed. We get married in New Delhi in early spring, within two weeks of meeting each other formally. There is no time to prepare for a wedding in Kashmir where things are too difficult anyway. I know this, but it does not prevent me from being sick at heart that the wedding is not being held in the valley. As I go about my errands my mind wanders off to all-night musical gatherings, midnight cups of fragrant green tea, hustle and bustle under colorful awnings, majestic mountain peaks against a clear moonlit summer night. I will have none of these at my wedding. I will have no dancers with sequined costumes and bell-anklets, no musicians singing their heart out as they play their ancient Kashmiri string instruments, nor will there be a tall thin old man with smoky blue eyes, their muse, standing up to applaud. There is a last long song the musicians sing that accompanies twilight until it becomes daylight, but no one knows it in New Delhi.

But we do make some music, we have a few *tumbakhnaris* hastily collected from local relatives, and some khos that we clang one on one as cymbals. We also have one kangri, but that is enough for the *isbandh,* and we happily seem to have plenty of that. We are bent on merriment, and so we make the most of it, singing our way through the musical nights leading up to the actual marriage ceremony. And we have the critical ingredient for a Kashmiri wedding, hordes of relatives, almost my entire tribe, all of whom have converged upon my father's house, traveling by car, train, and airplane. When my relatives are not carrying out assigned tasks they eat, sing, or gossip heartily, as they are supposed to do at weddings.

Someone remembers something and says, "The astrologer was right after all. He has lived abroad for fourteen years like Rama and he is beautiful like Krishna." Everyone agrees, their minds are at ease. They say this wedding was meant to be, nothing could stop it. There is no question that I shall now give up my career and follow my husband to the States. I have no doubt about it, either.

A few members of my husband's family are also present for the ceremony, but my family is present in full force. Our usual enthusiasm for a long drawn-out wedding is curtailed by Kishen's request for a short ceremony. Our priest looks askance at him, but upon receiving significant looks from my parents devises a shortcut. My family is as disconcerted as the priest at the synopsized wedding chants, but anything is better than a grown-up unmarried daughter, no matter what she does for a living. No one wants to raise an objection and hold up the proceedings. So instead of the prayers going on all night we are done by midnight, after which we go off to the hotel where my husband has made reservations for us.

We leave for the United States shortly after our wedding, after having spent our honeymoon arranging my visa. It looks as if it is just going to be him and me from now on as I wave goodbye to everyone at the airport. I hug my grandparents, aunts and uncles, and my parents and siblings; everyone is sad and relieved at the same time. They have no idea what lies ahead for me, but are assured by the fact that I have a good husband and I am capable of handling whatever turns up in the future. I am escaping by pulling away from shores with no land in sight ahead. You never leave home unless you are running away from something.

❊❊❊

We are careful as we start our married life in an apartment complex on the Philadelphia Main Line, next to a train station. My husband and I are two halves of a whole and we try to make our edges coincide, even when they sometimes do not, so that we do not leave gaps through which extraneous things may fly in, like insects on a hot evening. Everything is new enough for two people who hardly know each other, but there is the additionally surreal dimension of setting up home in an alien place. We buy utensils and essential goods, we decorate our interiors, then, exhausted, sit down on the new furniture and look about us. Everything is chosen by us and quite satisfactory, but we have no family with which to share our milestone. Our first new home is the joy only of our nuclear family of two. We are like the proverbial peacock dancing deep in a forest in the monsoon rains, plumage spread out like a gigantic fan in a rare celebration and there is no one there to applaud the show.

We do not remain two for long, thank God. The children come soon after.

First I am pregnant with my daughter. And then after five years I have another daughter. Like my grandmother and my mother I also remember the birth of both my children perfectly. When the first one came, I strained to see the infant in the steel crib on the side of the operating table, naked and kicking, unbelieving that the screaming little human being was the child I had been waiting for, for so long. Then I felt empty in my belly, a great emptiness where I had carried the child, fearful and bereft at the separation and yet relieved and tired.

171

My husband, equally thrilled at the birth of our daughter, was in a trance as he kissed me on the cheek like the father he had become. Then he went home to change and do the needful. A couple of juvenile nurses who were talking nonstop came in and scrubbed me down. They left immediately, without once looking in my direction as I lay there, cold and clammy, on the narrow long table. I started to feel a chill spread over my body. My voice was faint as I tried to ask them to give me a blanket. They were so busy with each other they did not hear me.

I ached for something to warm my limbs, and my back, but was too sedated and feeble to make a sound. I looked off and on at my baby daughter and smiled as she gamely battled the new forces of nature she encountered with her voice and arms and legs. Gradually, the caudal anaesthetic arose within my blood in a final wave and I slipped into a deep, cold sleep. I awoke much later in my hospital room, a little warmer under the regulation cotton blanket.

Through the window I could see the sky. The evening had turned to night, and the sky had turned to a dark purple, the color of longing. I thought of all the births in our family, the confinement room full of activity. For my aunt's deliveries there was always tea steaming in samovars in the corner of the room, relatives bringing sweet hard rolls covered with encrusted almonds and poppy seeds, gossiping in another corner, hot baths and spicy food. The astrologer was right about my life, I was doomed to live a world away from everyone. Being born a couple of hours late did not change what was written for me.

We bring our daughter home. A new person has joined us, her little mouth is all milky and toothless and harmless. Holding her and inhaling her smells and sounds is heaven itself. Well-wishers tell me that she has a temper but I do not see it; I have never found anyone so endearing.

Family members start showing up, more than willing to take an unnaturally long flight over oceans, all coming from India just to take stock of the new crop. The phone calls and the fat letters that we sent packed with photographs were fine, but they had to see for themselves. They could not smell or touch or gauge anything from eight thousand miles away. When it comes to children one always looks for signs and portents. As we sit together stories of birth and sometimes rebirth are retold. The mythology is infused with new blood and is perpetuated.

⚜⚜⚜

My mother-in-law has come to live with us for a while. She is expertly and serenely holding her brand-new granddaughter, whom she has anointed with a little charcoal gray mark from the cold ashes of our hibachi grill. The evil eye is the evil eye, the world is populated by human beings everywhere and children have to be protected. I tell her about the nurses and the cold bath.

She shakes her head with dismay at my birthing chills and says, "These chills could be with you forever."

She is telling me that no amount of spicy meatballs and cardamom tea can fix this terrible lapse on the part of the nurses.

"Why do they allow unmarried girls in a birthing place?" she asks.

At the apartment complex we young mothers have a play group. We meet regularly at the poolside, in a haze of peanut butter, chicken and celery and carrot soup, and diaper rash ointment. If the weather is bad we meet by turns at our apartments. We are quite clear about our objective, the children need to play with each other and we need adult conversation. We do not meet other than as a play group.

So, when one of the mothers comes to see me at my second-floor apartment I ask her in, delighted at the visit. No one ever comes to my apartment without calling ahead, and I am pleasantly surprised, having grown up with people showing up unexpectedly. We have some coffee; she does not like tea. Then, pulling something from her handbag, she says, "I have brought you a present."

It is a copy of the Bible. I say "Thank you" and set it aside. I already have a copy.

"Please read it and then we can talk."

"What would you like to talk about?" I ask, more than a little intrigued, although I am by now used to people asking me if I can tell them how Indians can marry sight unseen, or wear marks on their foreheads, or if my husband and I have Tantric sex.

"Well, I just thought that now that you have spent so much time with all of us you would like to change from your pagan religion to the true faith," she says earnestly.

"Why would I want to do that?" I ask, a little taken aback. "I am quite happy with my religion."

"Well, this is the true faith, you will see when we talk. Read it and give me a call when you're done. Feel free to ask me any questions you might have. You can even call me while you're reading the Bible—you don't have to wait until you finish. We'll have coffee and chat," she says this smiling all the time, as if I do not know what I am missing and am about to be given the biggest treat of my life. To me her eyes look a little glazed, but that could just be her false eyelashes.

I make another attempt to state my position.

"I don't like coffee. We are tea drinkers. I don't think you understand. I have deep respect for your faith and its history. Even if I accept your faith, I continue to belong to my faith," I say to her.

"Now," she takes my right hand in both of hers, "if I did not consider you a friend I would not be saying this to you. You must bring up a Christian family. It is the only way to save their souls."

I could be wrong, but there is a whiff of desperation in her voice. Perhaps she really does love me and wants to save all of us.

But this is too sudden. Someone I hardly know has pulled out something from inside me, leaving me bare, and is discussing it without my permission.

I reclaim my hand, a little unnerved by her unswerving single-mindedness. She can see it in my eyes, and now she is a little unsure and irritated at my ignorance. She moves to the edge of her seat.

I am a little testy when I say to her, "We are born into our religion. Besides, it's only three thousand years older than yours and followed by over a billion people." I am aware that I have stretched the truth by a negligible margin.

Now she is visibly annoyed. In her mind this is not a meeting of equals, this is a Christian confronting a pagan. She is standing up now, making for the door.

The clear warm honey in her eyes has turned cold and opaque, and her hand is on the doorknob, but she does not turn it yet. She has lost her initial zeal, but she is devout and will not give up without one last try.

"What is it called?" she asks.

"Hinduism," I say. It is a word coined by the British, and the one we now use as well. It is a convenient term. We used to call our religion "the traditional way"; we have neither a definitive book nor a single prophet.

She is silent but stares at me uncomprehendingly as she opens the door.

"Hindu-ism," I repeat, to make sure she hears me correctly.

"Never heard of it," she says as she shrugs and walks out. I close the door behind her, unsure if I am offended or amused.

I go back to my watercolors; I plan to do them again in oil. I paint whenever I have the time, which is not often because the girls keep me busy and I love it.

I never see the woman again, even at the poolside. No one seems to miss her much so I guess they know something that I am unaware of. Her church sends over people with progressively darker shades of skin color in an attempt at inducing familiarity, but I turn them away politely at the door.

After six years in the apartment complex we move to a house in New Jersey. This is where we have lived since. This is where the girls have been through nursery, kindergarten, grade, middle, and high school.

❀❀❀

The proselytizing woman was just another strange occurrence in our new world, and we put her away, scattered like bitter flowers among what was really important to us. Our main preoccupation is our daughters, whom we love passionately. In our anonymous and rootless world here they are literally our past, present, and future. My husband does not have anyone behind him, and I have left everyone behind. The children are at the center of our existence, our most precious possessions, nothing else matters. Anyway, I do not have any extended family, birthing herbs, or milk-mothers here. If we don't attend to them, who will?

When one has children one is very lucky, and we are beholden, we dare not be otherwise.

❀❀❀

My daughters made America home for us. We felt out of place initially in our new surroundings, but our daughters pulled us into the mainstream, feet first. When we arrived here we understood what it meant to lose your caste when you crossed the ocean. You lost your place in the world order. You could not carry your kinship, your ancestry, and your place in your society with you. It made no sense in another place, particularly here in the United States where people move vertically and horizontally in the flash of an eye. Lineages good and bad are best ignored, and neighborhoods are constantly changing.

However, as the girls grew up they helped us put down our bags and find our place. When I first arrived here it was a terrible feeling, to go from just being myself to jumping outside my skin and remaining there to view myself as a curiosity. When we went home for vacations, there was an ease I saw in family in India that I did not always feel here. As a new immigrant I was constantly seeing myself from the outside, as if I were in a play. My husband felt a little more at home in America, having lived, studied, and worked here for many years. Fortunately the children arrived just in time and we forgot about ourselves and concentrated on them instead, and it was a relief. As they grew they brought America into our house.

We have happily accepted and collected all the rituals and ceremonies brought to us by our children and they have taken some of ours. On Halloween nights when I go to the supermarket to buy candy I often tell myself that this is much simpler than cooking a four-course meal for a hungry *yaksha,* topping it with a raw carp, and carrying it up a rickety granary ladder for home delivery. I make sure I get my copy of the variable Kashmiri calendar due every New Year's Day, which for us falls in spring, so that I can make khichri on the yaksha day. But it's only for us. Our yakshas, native spirits of eternity, remained behind, unwilling to leave home as readily as we mortals did.

Our girls enjoy Shivratri, especially the part where they are given cash gifts to initiate prosperity; money brings money we believe. The girls also took Diwali to the school in the shape of a favorite holiday sweet, an instant winner with their classmates, judging by the requests that followed in ensuing years. In fact, I think that there are two homerooms in our school system that have grown up with a craving for *halwa puri,* fried whole wheat breads and cream of wheat dessert. We enjoyed the whole process and watched incredulously as our children filled our days. The girls are as rigid about their holiday menus as we were in Kashmir. We have the same Thanksgiving meal every year, and the girls find the omission of a single "fixin'" quite unforgivable. Christmas is also celebrated in all its secular splendor in our house. It has been a two-way traffic, a uniquely American phenomenon.

There is a point beyond which I am in unfamiliar terrain and my children are like foreigners to me. So I keep some thoughts to myself, believing that when the time comes my daughters will realize everything themselves. I am very careful not to say the things that Indian parents tell their children in India, because we live in America. Parents and children cannot take each other for granted here, whether that is a good or a bad thing only time will tell.

There is no question of my asking my daughters to follow Kashmiri rites of passage such as having their ears pierced. Ironically, in time, along with mehndi, bindi, anklets, and other Indian fashion dictates, American ears began to be pierced in profusion. And it is not only ears that are pierced, unthinkable body parts wear earrings now. My daughters have a couple of earrings in each ear, but they do not have the marriage part of their ears pierced, nor, like me, are they likely to do so. I cannot pull their earrings and ears and them close to me at will, as my mother and grandmother did with me. They are wary of having their space infringed upon, even when there are only four of us in a commodious house. My children are worthy great-granddaughters and granddaughters and daughters. But I cannot as a matter of course make preparations for their future lives under my roof. We have a different sort of attic here.

Still, we are a close family and it shows up in unexpected

ways. One day I was busy in the kitchen cleaning some carp I had found in the Chinese supermarket. My younger daughter was in high school and my older daughter was away at college. As I worked at the kitchen sink, scaling the fish, sending shining trajectories all over the kitchen and the floor tiles, I remembered my mother and the fish heads. Like her I had never cooked at home. Homesickness, dire necessity, and the absence of cooks helped me overcome my dread of skinning chicken, or cutting up raw meat and whole fish.

The doorbell rang, it was my younger daughter, and when I opened the door she was whistling "Hail to the Chief." She had just been elected student president, a post she would keep for the rest of her high school years. I gave her a hug and kiss and re-membered being elected student president at my college and then losing the election because of a vote-counting mixup. It was not the first time in politics-ridden Kashmir that forces other than democratic determined an election outcome, cir-cumventing the natural flow of things. But that was ages ago and I have a fresh carp to fry. So I return to the kitchen.

I pat the fish in a salt and turmeric mixture and then fry it to a crisp golden brown. My daughter, the student president and varsity athlete, settles down at the kitchen table to a hot fish–cold rice lunch. By the side of her plate is the inevitable stack of comic books she reads at the dining table. As I watch her eat I can see my mother and grandmother on either side of me and we smile at each other with contentment. My daughter is one of us.

خ خ خ

When they were much younger our daughters used to look for similarities between us and their parents' friends. Ultimately they saw us as their quaint but lovable Indian parents. In a sense we were at liberty to be as strange as we wanted to be, it was all attributed to our nationality. We were comforted by the fact that everyone their age seemed to be skeptical about their parents' ability to comprehend anything. My children felt our abilities were hindered even more by the fact that this is not India.

Sometimes I think I saw a certain disappointment that we are not light-haired and light-skinned like almost everyone else here. It had more to do with wanting their parents to blend in with everyone else rather than a feeling of racial inferiority. I did not tell them that even if everyone looked alike we would still have found something to kill each other about. They were not at a time in their lives when they wanted to hear the truth.

Our children told us that they were glad our marriage was one thing they could count on. They used to come back from school every other day with another divorce or separation story and it shook them up. After some time they decided that we are not susceptible to that sort of thing. I suspect that this kind of unquestioning family belonging served them well when everything else around them was nebulous. They felt that they had something over their American friends; their parents may be weird, but at least they could count on them to stay together. I did not tell them that divorce is becoming common even in India.

We don't think we are weird; we are just homesick sometimes. On weekends we listen to South Asian radio stations playing songs we sang as teenagers on a mountain camp, we seek out our special groceries, we watch movies that even we find outrageous, all this just out of longing.

When I listen to film music from India my younger daughter, the musician, says, "Mom, this woman sounds like a cat in heat."

I hold my tongue between my teeth and shake my finger at her as if she is being blasphemous. These singers are almost up there in our pantheon with our gods, even if we don't think they are so divine. It is an irrational bond.

Being Indian is a habit we cannot seem to shake off.

Neither can our children shake off their desire to be American. We grew up wanting to be like our parents, but our children want to be just like their friends. The peer group here is far more important than the trinity of Vishnu, Brahma, and Shiva, or grandmothers and goddesses. This is the driving force of the young here, the energy of their cosmos. It tears them from the arms of their homes and hurls them into an unmerciful wilderness where they twist and turn looking for the right direction. It is a wilderness with a religion all its own and is neither American nor Indian nor Hindu nor Muslim nor Christian. There are no jagged mountain peaks to show our children where they are. It is difficult for us to understand why trust and well-being have fled from the safety of family life into the chaos of wide-open spaces.

When my daughters were younger they loved our recollections of a time and a world far removed from theirs. These were their bedtime stories, tales more fantastic than any of their books could dream of. But they took the bedtime stories of an Indian home in America for granted and rarely wanted to know more. Things changed when they were asked questions at school, and they became less complacent and more interested in their Indian origins. Sometimes the questions they were asked carried an undertone of sarcasm and they could see it. Then they asked us about our dress, our eating with our fingers, the dots on our forehead. Then they wanted to dig a little deeper, they wanted to understand their identity and place between two disparate cultures. My children had a totally different set of concerns from the ones we had at their age and I think we grew up more carefree.

My husband and I have had to find answers to questions we did not even know existed. We never dreamt that we would have to justify and explain things that made us proud and happy. But that was before we left home to migrate.

As much as we might like to blend in we are a little different, its an old disease and cannot be cured. We come from a place where people hardly think of even their grown children as separate persons, with different goals for their well-being. Here every new baby is an individual, and we have to explain ourselves to our children. They think they are free and don't know that eventually they will come looking for us, and for those before us, no one is really free, and it has nothing to do with being Indian.

"We consider ourselves lucky to have you," I say to my daughters. And I say silently, "Wait until you have children of your own."

I am grateful that we managed to spend some summers together in Kashmir, even though that was years ago. We walked through the narrow lanes of the city, went up to the mountains, traveled to the lakes and the rivers. As I showed my children all my beloved places I gave them what I knew, a native's gift of gold. I thought to myself, like an old freckled cook with ginger eyebrows, "What will they remember?"

The last time we were in Kashmir was in the mid-1980s just before all hell broke loose. After a long memorable holiday with our family we took a taxi from Srinagar to Jammu. We were going to stay for a few days with my brother at Jammu and then take the train to Delhi to stay with my sister before flying back to the States. My brother, the doctor in the family, was posted in Jammu and my sister, carrying on her hereditary profession of teaching English at a college, lived with her family in New Delhi.

I wanted my daughters to absorb the manifold Kashmir ranges in all their shapes and undulations, in all their alpine hues and temperatures. It was something to breathe in icy Himalayan air in the morning and then experience the contrasting dust and heat of summer in the plains later on in the same day. We drove through two entirely different geographical regions. The girls found the hair-raising altitude of the winding road adventurous, but their chief excitement was reserved for the time they would spend with their cousins. They were about five and ten years old.

We left from my husband's house. On our way out of the city we passed my father on his morning constitutional along the golf course, and said farewell to him again. With his gray mustache, and his favorite cardigan and tweed peak cap, he looked very much the military man that he still was even after many years of retirement. As the taxi sped away I turned around to look at him. He was marching briskly with his chin up, inhaling the early morning air, and his only concession to age was the walking stick he held firmly in his hand. I continued to look out of the rear window of the taxi until he was a spot on the long road leading to his father's house.

When I could not see him at all I turned around and looked ahead to our journey. The next village was the saffron hunting ground of Habba Khatoon and her lover-king. The prospect of a full day's drive through the mountains on a sunny summer day with familiar stops for lunch and tea was wonderful. The journey from Srinagar to Jammu although about twelve hours long seemed much shorter because of the mountains and an equally tall story the driver told us. He said that America was fighting the Russians through the Afghans in Afghanistan and that some of the Afghan mujahideen had spilled over into Kashmir. The taxi driver's colorful version of the Great Game seemed entirely too imaginative, but it helped take our minds off the stupefying sliver of road we were navigating. As the man talked my husband and I exchanged glances that said silently, "Cock and bull story." The taxi driver obligingly took a photograph of us at the point where we truly left the valley behind and approached the flat road leading to Jammu. We promised we would be back next year. That was fifteen-odd years ago.

My brother and his family were not the only reason for us to stop at Jammu. I could not forget a story about a child goddess, or a recurrent dream about an insurmountable mountain. The dream just refused to go away. This was the pilgrimage I had promised myself as a cure.

The shepherd's story is known to all of us.

"'Tell my story,' says the little girl in the red and gold skirt.

"She smiles at me, a simple shepherd on a mountainside. I come here every day with my sheep and watch them graze as I lie half-asleep in the sun on the grass. I push my cap back from my eyes now and then and lift my head to count the sheep to see that none has fallen over the edge into the valley below. Today when my glance went northward toward a particularly precipitous side of the mountaintop, I was blinded. An incandescent figure in red and gold came out of the blue sky behind the mountain. As it moved toward me I saw it was a little girl riding an orange tiger.

"She was in front of me in what seemed a flash. When she smiled and took my hand and bade me follow her I knew who she was. She walked a few steps and pointed out a cave with a huge rock inside. The only way I could get in was to curve my body over the rock so that I would fit into the tiny space between the wall of the cave and the rock. I slid ever so slowly sideways until I reached a place where there were three small rocks. I knew this is what I was meant to find.

"I turned around to look for the little deity but she was gone. Somehow I found my way out at the other end and walked out into the open, and then back toward the spot where I had been watching my sheep. I have gone to the same spot for years but have never seen the cave before."

The shepherd said, "It was a dream, I thought to myself. Too much sun and loneliness. Too much time spent with rocks and sheep on a silent mountaintop. Then I lay down again at my accustomed place, and stretched my legs, and was about to put my cap back over my eyes when she appeared again. She smiled, and even when I closed my eyes to make sure that I was not dreaming

I could see her standing there, smiling at me. I opened my eyes, and she whispered in the purest voice, 'Tell them my story.' The mountains echoed every word she had said, and they rang in my ears until I had told everyone about her."

Straddling the Jammu mountains just outside the Kashmir valley is the cave shrine of the Mother Queen, the goddess of the tigers. Here she is the consort of Vishnu, red and gold and commanding as we pilgrims pant and rush up the mountains to seek her as fast as we can. She carries us all, robust and infirm, virgin and pregnant, male and female, all shouting, floating upward toward her sweet gaze as if gravity were nothing to us. Victory to the Mother, the Lady of the Tigers, the goddess Vaishno, we scream out to her, waving our arms as if we are carrying banners. We are drawn as if by a gigantic magnet and can only rest when we reach the top. We bathe in the ice-cold spring at the top of the mountain and then we enter her cave, most of which is occupied by a gigantic rock. We have to slide sideways to reach the *sanctum sanctorum.*

For years I have dreamed that I cannot make the last few steps to the top of a mountain. I knew nothing about the shrine then, but as I climb up with my husband I realize this is the place I have been dreaming about. We bathe in the spring, and make our way through the cave, lizardlike, curving our bodies over the rock, arms spread wide, taking tiny steps. The goddess comes into view ever so briefly and we come out at the other end, baffled like the shepherd. Something about the evanescent experience sends it straight to your subconscious and it remains there.

My recurrent dream vanished.

We returned home to America. Soon after we arrived we realized we should have given our taxi driver more credit and listened to him more carefully. The Afghan war exploded on the front page of newspapers here, as the driver had predicted. Russia, Afghanistan, Pakistan are just a stone's throw from my valley and the mountains carry news and trouble faster than it would appear.

Within a short time Kashmir also started deconstructing at an incomprehensible speed and the violence there became a regular part of the news. The schoolboys on the mountaintop, conscripted in childhood, and fed with an imported version of religious zeal, had finally been organized into an underground army with pay and munitions. The valley was saturated with Kalashnikov rifles, smuggled surplus from Afghanistan, and every other young Kashmiri was a militant. For a valley that within living memory trembled with one onslaught, we became remarkably inured to violence, all in the span of a decade.

We sent the marauding Afghan tribesmen back in 1947, but others from Afghanistan and other parts crept back in their place. They had all come to liberate Kashmir from infidel rule, preaching abhorrence of saints and shrine worship, beauty and art, music and love poems, all of which were mother's milk to us Hindus and Muslims.

Hindus of all varieties as well as Muslims perceived to be indifferent to the uprising are on "hit lists" written up by any one of the dozens of insurgency groups. The prevailing argument is, if you are not with the movement you must be against it, and you must be removed.

As we read the papers in the days and months after our return it was hard to imagine that we had just spent a glorious summer in Kashmir. Although we were aware of the disaffection and tension in the valley no one expected it to be caught up so suddenly in a destructive whirlwind. Kashmir blew up in every one's face when they were not looking.

The life we had together now belongs to the dreamtime of some bygone native peoples.

One morning my bedroom door is cautiously opened by my older daughter who wakes me up to say that Mrs. Gandhi has been assassinated. I prop myself up on my elbows, trying to open my eyes. She has a newspaper in her hand and she looks just like me at her age.

"Where?" I ask, as if it matters.

"In her garden. She was taking a walk."

Reading newsprint from cover to cover must be a genetic thing, I think, as I sit up in bed, slowly. Several scenes flash rapidly through my mind, like flashes of strobe light in a discotheque. It is early morning but my mind is dark and flash-lit alternately.

It is the mid-1950s. I can see Indira Priyadarshini, Indira Beloved to Behold, young and married, in an ankle-length red skirt and blouse embroidered with mirror work from the deserts of Rajasthan. She is in a houseboat in Kashmir, her hair is up in a fashionable knot and she is wearing red lipstick. A handsome man, her husband, is standing very close behind her, as if he knows that all too soon he will lose her to an unforgiving political wilderness. College girls, among them my aunts, are looking at the young couple with unabashed envy and adulation. It is a sight to dream of and to tell, beauty, love, and power all in one woman. A few years later we hear that Indira has broken every tradition and returned to her father, taking her two small sons with her.

Then, it is the summer of 1962. I see a father, a dutiful daughter, and two grandsons in white oxford shirts holidaying at a hallowed spring.

Many years later there is a son's wedding, and a mother–Prime Minister makes a whirlwind appearance with selected members of her cabinet and staff. I am the friend of a friend of Rajiva Gandhi, sitting on the periphery of the event. I can hear the sound of raw silk as Mrs. Gandhi walks past briskly, her back is toward me. It is difficult to say where the peach-colored silk blouse ends and her skin begins, but she has not worn lipstick for many years now, her graying hair is cut short in a formal style and her glance is scathing. She is her father's daughter, but the child is much more potent than the old man. A quick rustle back and forth among a few guests and Indira Gandhi goes back to the Parliament to conduct the family business. The wedding proceeds without her as the bride is adorned with flower jewelry.

Then, I see a deflated politician and she as fury incarnate, with her feet on all his roses, which she has deliberately torn apart, rose by rose, into a heap of petals. Soon after Mrs. Gandhi, now a pale mother, looks at the wreckage of the plane her favorite son, Sanjay, was piloting. There is not a glimmer of emotion in Mrs. Gandhi's frozen weary face, but you only have to see her eyes to see her loss. Now I hear that she is lying crumpled in the kind of rose garden from which her father was presented the perfect rose that he wore in his lapel every morning.

After Mrs. Gandhi's death her firstborn, Rajiva, hesitatingly accepts her Prime Ministership, only to be annihilated by a terrorist bomb at a public meeting.

On a bizarre day near the spring gardens of Chashma Shahi two college girls gate-crashed the Prime Minister of India's holiday. Neither could imagine that out of the four members of his family, only Pandit Nehru, the disciple of Mahatma Gandhi, would die a natural, nonviolent death. The Royal Spring Garden of Dara Shikoh might as well be in heaven now, Kashmir is not the easiest place to get to. Like Nehru's family everything in his ancestral valley is smashed to pieces.

"Did you ever meet her?" asks my daughter.

I think I have told my daughter these stories, but she can sense that I may want to talk about it. And like me both girls like to hear some stories repeated.

I tell her that I saw Mrs. Gandhi on several occasions. There is a knot in my stomach all day, for Indira Priyadarshini, for what she was and what has become of her. I mourn her, and the world I have lost in Kashmir, the one into which India is slipping, the distance I am from all that I know. The center has not held at all, and everything seems to be spinning out and far from everything else. Even so, I must look back and see where I have come from. There are real things even in an unreal past that I need to gather and carry with me wherever I am, if I am to keep my bearings right.

Both our daughters are adults now. The older one went on to graduate school and is now an excellent editor at a news company. The younger one is at college. They are mostly American children outside the home and Indian and mostly Kashmiri inside. The news from them is not always good, but they keep us occupied with good and bad news, and they are everything to my husband and me. They walk a difficult road, because they want to negotiate the fine line between our traditions and life in America.

There are some traditions that I pray they will keep, I do not want them to be lost in space where I cannot find my way to them. If they ever get married I have kept two each of my best shawls, two new and two antique, for both of them. I have kept my wedding ornaments for them, and if the time comes I hope they will wear them like me without having their ears pierced, over their ears like a horse. If they ever do ask me I will tell them about always having two wedding ornaments, one for each ear, about balance and harmony in life.

We have our large home all to ourselves now. Just as I left Srinagar and moved on, so have my children gone to live their adult lives, only with much less heartache.

What I forgot to pass on to my daughters they learned from their paternal grandmother, who eventually came to live with us in America. They had the greatest admiration and affection for the old lady because of her joy and her fearlessness even under the most challenging circumstances. She won their unshakable faith in her ability to conquer all on the day she captured a pesky yellow jacket that was terrorizing them. The girls were two and seven years old then. Their grandmother caught the bee in her bare hands and then released it to the winds. She would have risked anything to protect her grandchildren and to make them strong.

My mother-in-law conquered a great deal in her life, but she could do nothing about her heartbreak and longing for her home in Kashmir, her routine, her vendors, and her neighbors. She is gone now, having died peacefully in a Buffalo hospital, surrounded by her children. It was the thick of winter, and cars were slipping and sliding as involuntarily as the horses on the icy roads of Kashmir.

She was reassured at the sight of her children who had collected around her bedside; her daughter had flown in from India. Yet her face betrayed the homesickness that was eating away at her; she would have given anything to go home just once. She, always house-proud, used to say that she would like to go home at least once to have the furniture dusted, the house cleaned, and to have everything sorted out.

"Everything must be covered with dust, my carpets, furniture, everything," she would say ruefully, hoping to move us into sending her back home.

Naturally, we could not let her go, as old and delicate as she was. We did not want her to find out what we had hidden from her all these years, that her house had been robbed bare by militant crowds out on a rampage against the homes of Kashmiri pandits. The neighborhood she wanted to go back to is now a battlefield, the stomping ground of rebels and the army troops. Regulation boots clap down rural alleys and narrow cobbled lanes and courtyards in the old city where neighbors talked for hours regardless of their religions.

The city is not unfamiliar with firearms now, or with the idea of young and old carrying weapons, just like the tribesmen from Pakistan had done. Foreigners have sprung up everywhere like unfamiliar trees and no one asks who sent them or why they came. No one seems to mind violent strangers in Kashmir anymore.

The government of India comes down ruthlessly but unsuccessfully on the militancy. It is letting everything go from bad to worse, and the hatred of the masses for Indian troops and their tactics multiplies. There are so many examples of mismanagement, humiliation, and shortsightedness by the Indian government that even sympathetic Kashmiri Muslims are disgusted. Everyone is talking and everyone can hear what is being said, but no one is really listening. The militants have come back from training camps in Pakistan and Afghanistan with veins bursting with hatred and violence. The peaceable calm of an ancient way of life sounds nonsensical to them.

❦❦❦

The person who brought us the news about my mother-in-law's house said, "Everything is gone. You do not even need a broom to clean up. There is nothing there."

She is not the only one to lose her place in her neighborhood. All Hindu homes are a prime target for destruction by burning, looting, and desecration.

The mobs emptied my mother-in-law's home because they were exacting revenge from India for the events that had mauled the valley. She would have cringed at the mere mention of these atrocities, and hardly considered herself anything but Kashmiri. She participated in the marriage negotiations and then the weddings of all her Muslim neighbors' children, saw their children have children, and then fed those infants by hand when they paid her visits.

After the ravages of the mob the door to my mother-in-law's

house was broken down by the Indian security troops who moved in and have been there ever since. They are using her empty house as a lookout. This is what we heard from stray travelers who happened to walk past the house. The red roses she had trained on her high stone wall and the front balconies of her house, three stories high, were in full bloom in the summer, they said.

"The only reason the house is not burned down is because it is built of bricks, stone, and cement concrete," they said.

My husband's mother had the best treatment she could receive at the Buffalo hospital; the doctors were Kashmiri Muslims and Hindus, colleagues of her younger son, and students of her husband at the Kashmir Medical College. When she started fading they acted more like family than as doctors and refused to remove the life support systems. They called her "Mother" because she loved them like her own sons and daughters. I suspect that to them as to us she was a relic from a golden time in Kashmir.

The first thing my mother-in-law did every morning was greet the sun with a prayer. On her last day, as she lay dying, the evening sun set the clear, cold blue sky aflame, like a pyre. The minute the setting sun slipped from sight she slipped away with it. I could swear the sun had come for her on a fiery chariot, and even as we stared at the monitors she sped into the sky with him.

While I have been busy building a life here the old life in Kashmir has crumbled. Letters from home are milestones of an evaporating past. No remedy is in sight and everyone is singing the same incoherent song pattern.

Perhaps it was the passing of my mother-in-law and the wanton desecration visited upon her home, but I dreamed one night that every shop in the market in Kashmir was a butcher's shop, masses of meat piled up on every counter. We Kashmiris consider it terrible and portentous to see raw meat in a dream. I remember being told as a child to repeat frightening dreams in front of running water. That washes away the dream and prevents it from coming true. I try to repeat what I saw in the downstairs bathroom, but it turns my stomach as I tell the running faucet. The day is too beautiful and I try to lose myself in it, but my dream lurks in my mind like a hardened pariah dog that will not be shooed away.

I have another letter from home. My mother's mother is very ill and has been brought to New Delhi. She cannot be left by herself in her rambling house, particularly in winter. There is complete mayhem in Kashmir. Kashmiri Muslim militants have been killed by the troops who are on tenterhooks, beset by snipers, foreign terrorists, and a hostile population. Hundreds of soldiers have died in bomb blasts and counterfire by the insurgents. The shopping square where we used to go shopping for shoes, vegetables, and silk and wool fabrics measured out carefully with a cane yardstick is reduced to rubble.

"We try to carry on as if things are as they used to be but every violent day drags Kashmir back to the present," says the letter.

A marriage party is making its way through the lakes. Children are dragging their hands through the water to catch the lotus leaves as children have always done. The parents are busy cooking or playing cards, the women are singing wedding songs and burning wedding incense in their kangris when they hear blood-curdling screams from the children who rush inside, frenzied, shivering, and shaking their hands as if possessed.

The adults run out and look out at the water, and find dead faces looking at them from among the lotus flowers. By now the boatmen have also seen the floating corpses and have pushed the boat out into the clear lake, away from the horror. The wedding party silently comforts the children. The waters have been defiled, and a feeling of hideous gloom pervades the wedding boat. It is true, the talk of rebel Muslim boys being tortured, shot and then thrown into the lakes by government troops.

The feeling of unreality increases with each story that reaches us. We hear of midnight ferries and secret treks across mountain ranges. It is said that all Muslim households are expected by the mujahideen to watch videotapes smuggled in from Afghanistan. The tapes are a step-by-step introduction to insurrection training, detailing utterly inhuman practices which include flaying traitors. These are the only tapes Kashmiris are allowed to watch; all other entertainment is banned. It seems too outlandish to be true.

There is no single faction or movement; every neighborhood seems to be under a different guerilla leadership and Kashmiris obey several competing parallel authorities, if only to preserve themselves. Frightened tourists have kept away, and closed shops and lost revenue creates even more misery. Kashmiris hardly buy anything except necessities. Going out of the house for any but the most serious reason is foolhardy because of sniper attacks; you could just get caught in the crossfire. The militants are not hiding in the forests anymore.

The streets on which we children of all religions walked carefree to school have become deadly. Beautiful bridges that spanned the Jhelum for centuries, shopping promenades of antiquity, are patrolled by beleaguered troops who secure the bridges with little sandbag dwellings on either side.

The gaiety of summer in Kashmir is a tale we shall tell our children, because the likelihood of it ever returning in its original form is gone. Curfews blacken the most beautiful blue-green days, people run to stock up and catch up before yet another round of firing and insurgency. Kashmir is covered under dust from bombing and shelling, fires and killings. One thing has led to another, and the Kashmir I knew is dying as if it were set on fire and flooded consecutively.

No longer is the gossip about imminent weddings. Now in Kashmir they tell stories of pillage and plunder, of ancient shrines set afire, the worst fear of a valley steeped in wood-based architecture. We have to import vocabulary to deal with our plight, and its now commonplace occurrences. It appears that even grandmothers use the word "crackdown" with abandon. The rankness of destruction is all around.

There are so many theories, so many factions, and so much grief that it is futile to try to understand the metamorphosis.

Everyone stands accused: the government, the people, gods.

The Irish nuns are gone. They managed their life with great aplomb for years in an alien land where they did not even speak the language. But a political protest turned into a riot and the convent was set ablaze. It was not immediately clear which side the nuns were on, their preoccupations were suspect. The fire razed the convent to a pile of bricks and a smoldering golden cross. A new utilitarian-looking convent school has replaced the elegant old one; secular teachers have replaced most nuns now.

They say that even at the worst of times, mujahideen leaders delivered Shivratri supplies to pandits still living in Kashmir. Some say Muslim neighbors begged the Hindus not to leave, but they had to. I like to dwell on stories I can recognize, and though these are now improbable, I like to hear them repeated. That is the world I knew, but a story is a story and the truth is the truth. In Kashmir we say the Day of Reckoning is when falsehood burns to nothing and the truth becomes true.

One fateful day the valley bursts apart at the seams.

Frenzied crowds and neighbors have pulled Kashmiri pandits out of their homes and then systematically raped the women in front of their husbands and children. Then they brutally killed all the pandits who were left in the neighborhood, as they tried to take cover. One man hid in an oil drum and managed to escape but he saw the men in his family set afire like effigies; he watched them stumble and fall on their faces. He did not want to talk about the women and children. The man now lived in a refugee camp in Jammu but wanted desperately to go home and die there like the rest of his family.

In Kashmir men would not make eye contact with women, Hindu or Muslim, out of tradition and respect. Growing up in Kashmir I do not ever remember any disrespect from Kashmiri Muslims toward us just because we were pandits, quite an accomplishment by any standards, considering we were such a microscopic part of the population. We felt completely safe because our valley was our home. Kashmiri Muslims say the attacks on pandits are in retaliation for similar depredations by the army and police on their women and children. They say that the army has abducted men and women, there is no trace of some of these vanished Kashmiris. The troops have raped and killed, despoiled villages without mercy, the villagers are blind with rage, and Kashmiri blood is begging for revenge. Although there are no reported cases of the fast-diminishing pandits having dared to attack the Muslims, they pay the price for being considered synonymous with India.

Reluctantly the pandits leave the valley of their ancestors, looking for safety wherever they can find it. Their Muslim neighbors cannot help them even if they want to. Some of the pandits go to their relatives in other parts of India; some of them, erstwhile farmers, office-goers and householders, are housed in refugee quarters in Jammu. They try pathetically to reconcile themselves to the marginal lives of refugees in squalid camps, surrendering themselves to unfamiliar languages and weather.

We Kashmiris called ourselves the children of the Rishis, our godlike sages who exemplified the symbiosis of mysticism in Islam and Hinduism. We proudly forged a new philosophy and lived harmoniously in a tranquil valley. Now our pride is lost in the shallowness of battle trenches, houses razed to the ground, refugee camps, and the graveyards.

Almost all our relatives have come to New Delhi. Some have locked up their homes and handed the keys to the Muslims who have been their neighbors and friends for generations. They have fled in buses supplied by the government. Others have also been helped by Muslim friends who arranged a car or a taxi for them in which they escaped in the middle of the night. The truth is that the pandits cannot depend on honor any longer to see them through the times they are in. Honor loses its bearings when your tectonic plates are in flux.

Dhanna comes to stay with my parents and manages to survive until March. Then the summer heat arrives in full force upon the great plains of India, sucking Dhanna's blood dry; she wants to drink water every half hour. Snow and ice were nothing to her but she does not understand the parching wind of the *loo,* which dries out a newly washed towel in a matter of minutes. She gives up her struggle and never does see her home again. A Kashmiri's worst fears come true, she dies outside the valley, even if it is in her daughter's home. As Dhanna lay dying she looked lost. She knew she would never find her way home again.

It is natural that a mother sees her child born and the child sees her mother die, so my mother lets her mother go.

Soon after my cousin calls me in the middle of the night to tell me that Shyamji, my teatime and porch companion, has passed away. A week or so later I have a letter from my father, comforting me. He knows I have lost my best friend. My hold on Kashmir is slipping, the very ground on which I stood and from where I looked at everything is sliding away from under my feet. I have nothing in its place I can call my own.

The ancient culture of Kashmir, grown and nurtured for millennia on its beloved earth, is near extinction. The Hindus are gone and the Muslims are living under siege. It happened before our very eyes. Kashmiris can only hope for another miracle now. We cling even more fanatically to the legends that tell us how Kashmir rises anew from ruination every time. It may not happen in my generation, and it certainly did not happen for two of my grandparents, my mother-in-law, and hundreds of others who died in exile, grieving and homesick. It is of some comfort to me that Shyamji died before his Kashmir had started its infernal descent, and that he did not see the nightmares that came after him.

⚹⚹⚹

That was a few years ago.

Now things seem to have quieted down a bit. Tulli has gone back to Kashmir, for the first time without my grandfather. She has gone with my aunt and uncle, and I am so thrilled that she will be in her own house in Kashmir for the summer. I was born in that house, delivered safely in a riotous year by the same lady doctor on whose lap Mahatma Gandhi lay dying after being shot by a Hindu fanatic. We had fondly, if euphemistically, continued to call our home The Poplars, even when only one poplar remained to tell the tale of its drowned brethren. Miraculously, on my grandmother's return, she found her house waiting for her; it had not been occupied or destroyed by the troops or the militants.

I want to go home with my grandmother even as I sit in my family room here in America. I walk through the garden with Tulli; we are doing the rounds together as we used to do when we returned to Kashmir after a brief winter's stay outside the valley. The perennials are overrun by grass and weeds, yet they obviously struggled hard to survive, their faces persist through the predatorial growths. The rosebushes that unfailingly produced magnificent white roses with sweet petals year after year have grown enthusiastically but untrammeled. As a result their ardor has not added up to much. The roses have dissipated from lack of pruning and have to be trimmed down to a productive height. The house smells musty for want of airing.

We go through all the empty rooms, Tulli and I, opening the doors and talking. We climb up the wooden staircase, once carpeted with green and blue Kashmir kilims woven with red geometrical patterns, held back by black cast iron-rods in rings fitted into the steps. Now the carpet is bedraggled, but it is still there as we climb up two flights of steps to the third floor attic, opening all the windows and doors as we go along.

The attic looks as though it has been waiting for a long time for us to return. The straw ropes on which we hung vegetables to dry in the summer, and on which we hung clothes to dry on wet days and in the winter, are still there, but gray and dry from disuse. The wooden floors are covered with a soft layer of dust and are bare except for ceramic pickle jars standing expectantly in a row. The entire row of cream jars with reddish brown screw-on tops is empty, and unlikely to be filled.

It is clear from the look of the attic that no anticipated future events are in sight. Shyamji, the real spirit of his house is no more; the servants have fled. We climb down to the ground floor and turn left at the bottom of the stairs into the library.

I wonder about the books of my grandfather's modest library, now that no one lives in the house anymore. He never was very careful about keeping track of all the people who borrowed his books. His friend on the other side of the fence catalogued every book in his library and pasted printed bookplates inside the covers. The labels bore catalogue numbers and this quote from *The Tempest:* "My library was dukedom large enough." The grandchildren and great grandchildren of neither man can use their libraries with impunity now. The tempest has seen many dukedoms fall by the wayside in the interim.

Sudha Koul

The books in my grandfather's library constituted a most varied selection, ranging from Hafiz to Dickens, to *Sumran,* an anthology of Kashmiri verse, to my uncle's collection of socialist magazines, to Thomas Mann. The Persian book-oracle by Hafiz was in my great-grandfather's hand, simple calligraphy, illustrated with original paintings of his time. I remember that I so loved the paintings in the Hafiz book that I illustrated some of the text-only books we had. My favorite author at the time was P. G. Wodehouse, and his books particularly suffered from this indignity. I loved the golf stories, and when my husband played golf many years later I wondered how on earth I could have thought it was a humorous game. Later still, when my children drew pictures in their books I remembered, and contrary to popular wisdom did not prevent them from doing so.

My grandmother and I go from the library to the dining room which was always a little dark, even on the sunniest day. The wood dining table and cushioned chairs are in place, but the curtains made out of recycled, out-of-vogue saris have frayed from the seasons of our absence. One touch from my grandmother as she tries to open the window sends the dust flying and she has to sit down because she is overcome with coughing. I lean against the wall cupboard with the antiquated brass bolts and wait for her to recover. Then, a few minutes later she gets up and we walk from the dining room down the three or four brick steps to the connected kitchen quarters.

The kitchen is always colder than the rest of the house because it has a cement floor whereas the rest of the house has hardwood floors. The fish basket hangs expectantly from a hook in the wooden beams of the ceiling, its unalleviated sturdiness a testament to the reeds of my grandmother's ancestral village. Across the low ledge that marked the boundary of the kitchen, inside the shoeless part, a couple of kangris are where Tulli had placed them on the shiny steel kitchen table when she left. The frayed kitchen blanket in which she kept my lunch warm for me when I ran home from college, sometimes with friends, lies folded on top of the kitchen almirah. I look inside the chicken wire doors of the almirah as I used to when hungry and of course find no leftovers there. The austere red stripe on the chocolate-colored blanket is still vibrant. The kitchen fires that produced some well-known dinners have long since gone out and the hearth is dark and stone cold. The hearth and the kangris, and the steel table coexist in frigid uncommunicative silence, the old and the new, still refusing to recognize each other.

A couple from Kishtwar has been taking care of the house. Our neighborhood is relatively safe because of the telecommunications center nearby. The Kishtwari man needs his job, even so he is a brave man to risk sticking to an office schedule. He and his wife will attend to my grandmother.

The phone is ringing in New Jersey so I have to leave Tulli on her own in Srinagar. I call her up a few days later, dying to know everything. My grandmother said she passed the first night tossing and turning at the great emptiness surrounding the house. The next morning she got up, made some tea, and went outside to sit on the front porch. I can only imagine that her life must have passed before her eyes. She spent a better part of the morning drinking tea and staring at the snow on the Himalayan ranges riding the sky. When you grow up with snow, it is a thirst that must be quenched annually, and she has not seen snow for many years now.

Then Tulli heard the garden gate latch click open, once an oft-repeated and welcome sound. Not anymore. She sat up, petrified; she was not expecting anyone.

Through the arbor vitae she could see someone coming in, holding the garden gate ajar.

Then a piercing cry rent the morning sky, "Fresh fish, the most unique, the most sweet, the freshest fish."

The garden gate started to close slowly. My grandmother stood up and called out to the fishwife. The gate flung wide open and Fatha ran in. Dropping her kettle on the garden path she ran up the stone steps to my grandmother, and tearfully embraced her with a bony fierceness.

"Where have you been, my sister? Nothing is the same since you left," the fishwife wailed.

She beat her haggard breast, "Only my two youngest children are left, and I have locked them in the cellar. We have to eat. No one is safe, our life is hell."

"How did you know I had come back?" asked Tulli.

"I did not. I always stop here and wish I could see you just once again. I have been selling you fish since I got married, do you think I would stop now? Could I go past your house and not come in to greet you. The world is upside down, but are we not sisters? So what if you are not here?" said the fishwife.

There is a pause on the phone.

My grandmother says to me, "A lot of people are praying for a bird these days. A lot of people are looking to the sky these days hoping for a seed to fall. But for a different reason because this is a different time." She tells me that the river seems to have shriveled up in loathing at its desecration. There is no snow and there is no water. "Now we need a seed from the heavens so that the waters may rise again. Rice Blind is dead now, her houseboats rest on stilts. Her sons are nowhere to be seen," says my grandmother.

The fishwife knows the story about the bird, the seed, and the water. It is from the common mythology we all, Hindus and Muslims, share.

I try to re-create here in New Jersey what I can of what I knew. Sometimes when a summer day is as perfect as this one, I step down from the deck into the garden and walk around holding my hands behind my back and humming like my grandfather.

The Persian lilac we planted a few years ago has matured into a beauty and there is a gathering of butterflies hovering around it. It is a lovely sight to see multicolored versions of Vishnu the Preserver flitting about on the front garden, on the blood red impatiens flowering amid deep green foliage, and in this universal moment I forget where I am. What is missing in my re-created world is what makes it different, the snow line and the mountains, all the relatives and the laughter and the coming and the going.

When I talk to my aunt on the phone she tells me it's the same there in Srinagar as well, those days are gone, she says, but that piece of information is of little comfort to me.

"In Kashmir, everyone is trying to survive and to keep their dignity intact," says my aunt.

I feel lucky that I came away with a glorious picture in my mind. They say in India that a person who goes blind in the monsoon season always thinks of life as lush and green. But they also say that when someone kills a snake, the killer's face is forever etched in the eyes of the dead reptile.

๛๛๛

My husband brings in the newspapers from the driveway. I have made some breakfast for us and we read the papers as we eat. Another slippery slide into hell in Kashmir is reported on the front page. The latest news is that pilgrims to Amarnath and the crews attending to them have been massacred. The road to heaven is littered with corpses of all religions. Pahalgam is a killing field and the Liddar roars on, bellowing its outrage at the sacrilege.

I turn to the Internet for further details. A couple of clicks and a photograph pops up on the monitor. Pahalgam at the bridge on the Liddar where we college girls used to take off our shoes and put our sore feet into icy waters. Corpses lie scattered across the photograph. Women cry and beat their breasts and their screams are soundless. Men, women, children, villagers, of all religions, all trying to make a little money in a short-lived season, pilgrims on a long promised journey, all dead.

Kashmir is back into the beginning of time. The valley churns once again like a ghastly primeval soup. Will new life emerge from the brew in time? Will I be there for the new beginning, which I pray will come?

If you go away from the photograph, off the right of the computer monitor, and walk up the hill there is a small bakery. If you are early enough you will see the old baker with his four sons pulling out piping hot loaves of bread from the oven. If you go still farther up you will find a winding path that leads up to a clearing in the pine forest next to a small mountain brook. A log fence marks the almost level clearing, and this is where my grandfather loved to pitch tents and set up camp in the summer. By the time we reached the camp, huffing and puffing and thirsty after our climb, we were usually in dire need of the cold brook water.

Our family camp was large; we were so many and needed all the housekeeping help we could get. Still higher up is one of the old summer "cottages" of the Maharajah, the one that was requisitioned by our college camp. But all that is out of the picture now and all you can see is the bridge over the river and the carnage. The camera is interested only in the dead bodies, the dazed on-lookers and bereaved relatives.

It is foolish to expect good news about Kashmir when I open the newspaper, but I hope against hope. Like any lover, I am always starved for a glimpse, even if it breaks my heart. I am always looking for the word *Kashmir* in the news, but then so is every Kashmiri.

We meet here often, Hindu and Muslim children of the Rishi Var, the valley of our common sages, and there are plenty of us in the United States. At our get-togethers, which have decreased over the years, we have our green tea and Kashmiri food and talk to each other in Kashmiri, something we cannot share with anyone else. A single sentence in Kashmiri can reduce us to tears or laughter as no other language can. Even though we meet in the peaceable calm and orderliness of American suburbia all of us are thrashing about internally, for different reasons, redoing our inner maps. We don't talk much about the current situation in Kashmir, for the moment being Kashmiri is quite enough, and we all need that intrinsic affirmation of our identity. We still don't know exactly where the chasm is, and because we are on neutral ground, on the no-man's-land of another country, we carry on as if nothing has happened. We cling to periods of sanity with fierceness because we know that all too soon it will be followed by worse insanity.

Summer brings fall, which brings winter, and then it is spring all over again. I survive winter awaiting the spring arrival of tulips, crocus, daffodils, and hyacinths, all of which I coax with great difficulty and perseverance. A hairlike mesh of roots from the occidental maples that surround my house threatens every plant with suffocation. The maple looks like the chinar, but the chinar is a plane tree, a cousin perhaps of the sycamore and wears similar mottled bark. The crocus here also looks the same but lacks the saffron heart of its Kashmiri incarnation.

Its peony time on a late-spring morning. I am reminded of bridal couples under a wedding shawl, sanctified by an entire night of nonstop chants and prayers and burnt offerings. At this concluding wedding ritual, the couple is momentarily divine, and entitled to petals instead of complete flowers. Their families carry baskets of peony petals and shower them on the shawl covering the newlyweds until they look like a heap of petals. At that moment the couple is godlike, but the rest of their human life is up to them.

My husband and I have tried to do the best we could, but after that fleeting brush with divinity we are at heart only human beings. We have built a family here without any recognizable road signs. We came as immigrants, but have made ourselves at home by becoming firmly ensconced in our new seasonal merry-go-round.

Of course, you can never be a complete immigrant or completely domiciled, and one still carries one's hometown within one, in so many ways. After all these years, when my husband goes away on a business trip I can hardly sleep for fear and for the emptiness of the house. I sleep on the couch downstairs praying fervently that the midnight programs on television will be interesting. Then, remote control in hand, I wake up the next morning.

I wonder what will happen if I should die while asleep. No one will know I am dead until my husband comes home. My neighbors are not the inquisitive sort and they respect my privacy. Then I pray that if it has to happen it will be the night before he arrives so that I am not in an extreme state of decomposition. Then I laugh to myself. This cannot happen back home. But I live here now and that is that. When you have to do something you do it.

One winter in Kashmir, my friends and I were sitting with our feet up on a huge sofa under a blanket and we read a short story while we waited for dinner. It was about a pregnant housewife in America who was waiting for her husband to come home from work. I think his name was David. She put the electric kettle on because he liked to have his tea the minute he walked in or something like that. Something went wrong. I don't remember exactly what, and the woman was electrocuted, and as she was dying she thought of her husband not being able to have his tea on time.

We could not believe it, being used to homes filled with uncles and aunts and cousins and servants. Where was everybody, the neighbors, and the relatives? It did not occur to me, a teenager in Kashmir, that you could possibly live without someone being within earshot. America must be a very lonely and quiet place, very sad and very frightening. The other issue, that is, of a woman thinking of her husband's trivial comfort as she died terribly, did not bother me at all. When it came time for my marriage, it happened so quickly even I did not have time to prepare for it, or I would have remembered the story.

I am still not completely reconciled to the fact that I will have to live in a house with my children far away, without relatives and servants. I have no one except my husband with whom I would as a matter of course during the day conduct a conversation.

My neighbors are friendly, and we wave a lot to each other across the backyard and occasionally have a chat and seasonal get-togethers over barbecue grills. There is certainly no one here with whom I can share all the stories I have brought with me. I would have to explain too much and it still would not mean anything. It is the same for my neighbors, all of us are transplants, and some have deeper roots than others do.

When I sit on my favorite chair, looking out into the vast expanse of my backyard, I think about all these things. This house has been our home for the past twenty-odd years. We have sacrificed capital gains for continuity, putting down roots, and I think we may have succeeded.

We have some history in this house. We have seen trust and betrayal, love and hate, childbirth and children leaving home, we have had good times and bad. We have something more than just shopping for consumer electronics and making the house habitable. In the beginning we were embroiled with settling in as immigrants. Our house was new, a builder's sample when we moved in; no one's grandparents had lived in it. We used to have a houseful of shiny new unbroken objects. Now things are beginning to fall apart. The mortar and pestle are made of marble so they look new, but fortunately the kettle is beginning to turn black at the bottom. The brick walkway has become uneven with the rise and fall of the water level, but it is the only one of its kind, the one that leads to our house. The house has been a constant, like an old dog. We have grown a house spirit, and my husband and I, the adults, know what it looks like.

"So how is everything?" Izmat asks, as I hand her some green tea boiled in milk with crushed cardamom and almonds, Dhanna's favorite. Izmat and I are meeting after five or six years.

She still does not wear any makeup; she is as devout and austere as always, and her skin is perfect now. Her hair, not as gray as mine, has been in a hair clip for the last quarter of a century, but the severity of her hairstyle only accentuates her beautiful face. When she stopped wearing her burqa she replaced it with a chiffon veil that she wore like a scarf which covered only the back of her head. Now she wears a scarf Western-style over silk shirt and pants.

We have met after years, and we have been talking nonstop, trying to catch up on everything. We feel so young when we see each other. It is so easy to laugh together.

I ask her about her family and she tells me that though her father is no more, they are still in the shawl business, and her brothers still have the upscale shop near my grandfather's house. Izmat is full of chatter, and loves company, like her father, and like me. She remembers why I stayed at home when I had the children.

"Your mother scared the wits out of you by telling you all those stories."

She remembers that my mother had gone into a panic when she read that a baby-sitter in America had put a baby in the oven instead of the turkey. We never had to have any baby-sitters in Kashmir; everyone lived in the same house. But we did have our own peculiar brand of baby-disaster stories, having to do with hot samovars and boating trips.

Izmat has brought me three gifts. One is a packet from my grandmother from her last trip home. Some dried crushed mint leaves from my grandfather's well. In summer I make butter-milk drinks sometimes, and then I sparingly add a pinch of the mint. It cools everything. I could have laughed when my older daughter called me from college to tell me about the benefits of acidophilus yogurt drinks for women.

"The mint will have to last forever," I say, inhaling the refreshing fragrance of the green powder. "Who knows when I will be able to go home again."

Izmat smiles and does not say anything. There is nothing to say.

Her second gift is seed incense from a shrine. I don't ask her if the *isbandh* is from her shrine or from one of ours, a Hindu shrine with the steeples of a mosque, trusted for the miraculous powers of the smoke from its incense. It does not matter. We trust each other's mysteries even now in spite of everything.

"You will need isbandh when your children get married," says Izmat.

"God willing, yes, but where will I find chinar coals and a kangri?" I ask, half jokingly. I am skeptical about the part I will play in my children's personal lives. They are like seeds themselves; they have taken root wherever they have scattered. But it is good to have the incense. If they get married and I have any part to play in the wedding, I will purify the air with its smoke and fumigate the evil eye out of existence.

For the third gift Izmat has put herself in danger at the U.S. customs.

When I open the package of narcissus bulbs I am so incredulous that all I can say to Izmat is, "Do you know what an awful name they have here for narcissus? Paper whites. And they have the vilest smell."

She grimaces and smiles. We know that in Kashmir the perfume of narcissus can send you straight to heaven. I know these bulbs are from her garden, and whispers of our soil are caked on them. I am reminded of long brown feet and a rich straw sandal and a tall, dignified man wearing a white and gold skullcap.

I also remember a chorus of girls in an opera in our college auditorium. The narcissi of *Bombur Yemberzal* plaintively sing, their arms outstretched toward the audience, "Will not our garden be laid to waste by the seasons?"

The garden of which the flowers sang has almost been laid to waste but for me here, in my suburban American house, there will still be narcissus in the spring. When I plant the gift of the bulbs, the earth of Kashmir will be mixed in with the earth in my garden forever. The narcissi will lie silent in the ground and come spring they will appear from a melting earth, a perennial promise of rebirth after a frozen still season.

Izmat and I won the first prize at an art contest when we were in college, she for portraits and I for landscapes. The award was presented by the now titular head of the state, the only son and heir of the runaway Maharajah. It was a lot of money for two young women. We spent it on the same day by taking all our friends to Ahmed's restaurant on the Bund, a promenade alongside the river Jhelum. In summer Ahmed, called Ahdoo by everyone, put chairs and tables outside for his patrons. We sat under the chinar that was so old and wide that it took up half of Ahdoo's restaurant garden. Its branches spread over the garden, the promenade, even hanging over houseboats lining the sides of the river. Some branches almost touched the water.

We ordered skewered minced lamb kababs with mint chutney in the kind of quantity that only young people can eat, and finished up with sweet cream eclairs and chocolate pastries and pots of tea. The owner of the restaurant was a legend in his lifetime, and like his father before him, had cooked for the British Resident in Kashmir.

Now Izmat is a doctor with a successful practice. Many of my class fellows from the Government College for Women have, like Izmat, gone on to become professionals, and they can be found where there are professors, doctors, politicians, poets, engineers, publishers, and housewives. Many of them live in the States now, winning accolades that would satisfy even our exacting principal.

"It is not the same river anymore," says Izmat, sitting on my deck, sipping her tea. "The water has almost dried up. You can smell the stench of the weeds and the silt for miles. There is no drinking water." I prefer not to pay any attention to what she is saying, even though I have already been told about the water in Kashmir. There are some truths that I don't want to hear even at my age.

She looks over the deck railing into the garden and says, "The weather is so perfect today. You are very lucky to be living here."

I nod my head in agreement.

On a sunny day we Kashmiris are apt to overlook a lot.

Between us we know that the world we grew up in has vanished and we have to meet in objective spaces now. Izmat and I have a familiar dinner of fish and lotus root, and kohlrabi greens and rice. Everything comes to America on a platter and anything is possible here.

When I leave Izmat at the train station, we kiss and embrace, parting Kashmiri-style, no holds barred. Driving back I ruminate like millions of immigrants before me, and think about where I am, where I belong, and where I will be when I am old and undesirable. My house in America is built on the old training grounds of the British army. Before them the settlers lived here, and before them the Native Americans. I am the latest wave in a cycle of change, waiting my turn to be relegated to the dust of history. Is my past and everything it held gone forever? Is everything finished or will something survive?

We are at the Asia Society for an exhibition of discoveries unearthed in 1924 from the Indus Valley Civilization. The artifacts have traveled all the way from Pakistan.

Whenever I hear of a South Asian exhibit or event, if I can make it I do. It tickles me; this is new nationality, South Asian, forged for us by time, pulling us together when we have torn ourselves apart. The fact is that we are the same people. Our language, food, clothes, music, the things that make us laugh and cry are all the same. Ours is the only region in the contemporary world where all the heads of state have been women, at one time or another. We have something buried underground, but not yet excavated, that ties us together. I believe that although South Asia has been chopped and sliced, we have been pushed together again by our underlying forces, in time that lives in cycles.

We in South Asia were one of the first group of civilizations in the world but I have seen none of the archaeological finds that show our beginnings. Most of these are in Pakistan now. My excitement is quiet because I do not know what to expect. A couple of my childhood friends are married in Pakistan and they have often invited me but I have never been able to make the trip. The exhibit is billed as pottery and jewelry and statues from five-thousand-year-old ancient Pakistan, and is part of the celebrations of the fiftieth anniversary of its independence from Britain. First, we'll go to the museum, then we will go to dinner, and then perhaps a little jazz in the village.

I am reminded of a conversation with a cousin who recently visited Kashmir. She said that she had gone up to the Shiva temple on the crater, our favorite climb many years ago. There she found a young schoolteacher in a burqa explaining to her class that the temple was from pre-Islamic times. "We must know our history and this is part of our history," she smiled at her young pupils.

My cousin, a living part of the history of Kashmir, was standing just behind her.

The Museum is quiet and shining clean. Most people have left. We have seen our beginnings at the museum, terra-cotta, dice, my god and goddess, and their wild beasts. They are all there, in their earliest known, five-thousand-year-old manifestation. It has been a great and long-awaited sighting for me, but seeing the first depiction of the deities is numbing.

As we step into the rain outside my mind is a jumble. I celebrate the privilege of seeing the god and the goddess. But I wonder, what is true now, what was true then? Tigers, women, midnight wells, sacrificial lambs, one-piece lung-trachea-kidney-liver offerings, circling kites, and goddesses on mountain tops, all the things I had to leave behind in Kashmir? The golden goddess and the god I have just left behind in the museum, in glass cages, brilliant after five millennia of subterranean rule? I knew they were there somewhere, we had such vivid recollections of their power. All the figures are meticulously sculpted in filigreed detail or in bas-relief on seals. The work is so fine and sophisticated that it boggles the mind. How long have we had them?

I start when a hand clasps my right shoulder, a firm and sure hand. It is just my husband, but in New York you never can be sure.

"Time to go, maybe we can have dinner, forget the jazz and hit the New Jersey Turnpike. It is late," says my husband in my ear. This is his territory; he has studied and worked here for well over four decades. He knows the rules of the game and is completely at home in America. It is always quite clear to him what should be done. Nothing is confusing if you see it his way.

But I am fed at the gut by a long cord that goes over the oceans, over the mountains and finds nurture in a faraway valley. Try as I might, I have not been able to cut the connection and find anything else that satisfies my spirit and body as well as my own water and my own soil. My mind is muddy and full of turmoil, and I am so confused about the past, the present, and the future. Where do I belong? What do I tell my daughters? Where do they belong? Do we come from a community that no longer exists except in the minds of its people? Did we really have a cherished homeland where we lived carefree and content? How can you not be wanted in your own home?

I can hear my mother say, "The muddiest swamp produces the most splendid lotus, the flower on which the goddess of learning sits." She is oiling and combing my hair into two long plaits, an ideal time to pass on valuable information. The slow conversation and the comb with its teeth pressed hard on my scalp, moving in a soothing rhythmic pattern, ensures that wisdom goes into my skin along with the oil and nurtures me inside and outside forever.

"The lotus root comes up all the way from the native soil through the mud, through the mile-long weeds, and it takes only real things from its surroundings, drinks them up through its six veins and produces ruby lotus flowers and emerald leaves on top."

I nod to my mother, who is eight thousand miles away.

"Chaos is good, Mother. I will take only what is real from the murkiness that surrounds me," I say under my breath. I will not attract attention when I mutter to myself; in New York people talk to themselves a lot. Like my daughters who call me on the phone when things become really clouded, I call out to my mother on the other side of the world and hope my whispers will carry over the oceans. With mothers anything is possible.

My mother used to have to redo my braids until I felt they were identical, balanced equally, one on either side. She does not have to worry about that anymore. I have learned to live with many disharmonies.

The god and goddess have come to me at the right time, they knew exactly when to show up. They have existed as long as the living world has been half male and half female, and they will exist as long as that is true. As I had suspected, the power is equally divided between the god and the goddess, but the goddess is more fearsome. We have prayed to her with our own ideas of what she looks like. Now she comes to me, showing herself to be exactly as I thought she was, riding tigers, slaying demons and tigers, hair flying, extraordinarily powerful. I see a painting hanging from Dhanna's ceiling cornice. The goddess stands astride the Demon Bull Mahishasur whose decapitated head rolls in the dust under the paws of her tiger. As a child I was awed by the story and the painting, now I have seen the five-thousand-year-old inspiration for both. Thanks to careful Pakistani archaeologists the fearsome goddess has appeared when I needed her most, a symbol of continuity and resurrection, a lifeline to my beginnings.

Our native forces are alive and well and traveling the world. They have always been there and will find us wherever we are.

But things appear and disappear and then reappear.

Sudha Koul

Once the cycle is complete you have to start all over again, time is unending, there is no bottom line. Nothing is new, and that is all we know going forward.

❧❧❧

Kishen and I walk in the New York night, making our way to the parked car, and both of us are quiet.

We pass a crosscultural line of eateries on either side of us. I smile to myself when I pass "Indo-Pak" restaurants in New York, and I think of a nation split in two, battling each other ever since, and now rejoined in a New York café. I remember loving neighbors who did not eat in each other's homes. But in New York pure ethnicity is elusive, and you always end up making an evening of it. We will stick to our original plan, dinner and definitely a little jazz before we head home. The nuns managed to give all of us girls, Hindu and Muslim, a taste for Western music.

❧❧❧

I am busy with my work now, writing books and painting. I enjoy being at home while I pursue my vocations. Occasionally in the summer when the humidity is gone for a couple of days and the sun shines straight and dry, I open my trunk and spread out my pashmina shawls. Then I lie down on a deck chair and soak in the sun as well. The deck has lovely potted plants, and around it flowering trees and bushes have been steadily growing. On the wide wooden ledge are bottles of pickles packed tight in spices and mustard seeds. I can see the fermentation as bubbles of air rise through the red pickling mix and oil. It is an exquisitely familiar summer sight. My black hair is graying now, but my fierce craving for Kashmir must go into the pickling and compensate for red hair because the result is quite fiery. The fumes from the fermented mustard seeds could offer fair competition to a tough old man with a hookah pipe in the side of his mouth.

My daughters have moved into a new apartment and I have to ship a few things to them. I love taking care of their requests, which are becoming more and more reasonable every year. They are hardworking women and it gives us peace of mind to know and trust that when we are not there for them they can put bread on their table. They are not our possessions nor are they likely to be anyone's property. And, as much as I understand what a complete overturning of the old world that entails, it's a welcome and comforting notion.

But first some time for myself on this lovely day. I must go out on the deck and dry out any remaining mildew from my bones before the winter. I make a pot of tea, heat up milk to a boil in the microwave, what a blessing, and settle down on a chair on the deck. It is a nice feeling, finally to be available only to the gods. It is one of those days when I feel as though there must be the tiniest space between the soles of my feet and the now curving wooden planks of the deck.

The tea is perfect. It is my own blend of full-leaf teas, a little of this and a little of that, with some everyday tea for body. I pour myself a cup and settle down to the weekend paper. I am more or less at peace, and seem to have finally accomplished my mother's goal of being "settled." But everyone has djinns they house. In the midst of my American life I am still kept awake some nights by my birthplace, tormented by the twisted turn of events in Kashmir. Life there seems cruel and fantastic in contrast to the streamlined suburban life I see outside my double-paned insulated window in New Jersey. It was not so long ago that we had a beautiful life in Kashmir.

Now the news from Kashmir differs from month to month, and sometimes it even looks as though a resolution is in sight. On every wound a crust of some sort must form, but it is not a guarantee of healing. There are intermittent reports of normalcy, the institutions are working, people have long, drawn-out weddings when they can. Some cultural life is back, even though the movie houses are still out of commission. The moral police have retreated from their oppressive ways. Even the tourist trade is trying to edge back to life, each successive tentative season. Some Kashmiris are building houses, trying desperately to live decent lives. As homesick as ever, a handful of Kashmiri pandits have trickled back to their homes; you can probably count them on one hand. Everyone hopes that time will come full circle again, like a dog's tail.

I think most of us carry on hoping for the best, or sometimes even the impossible, a resolution to everyone's satisfaction. We get a couple of weeks of quiet. Then the next week there is news of anarchy in the city square or of tourists being kidnapped or killed and reality stares us again in the face with a horrifically superior grin.

The cycle repeats itself.

Not everyone will benefit from peace, I think to myself.

I flip open the pages of the crisp newspaper and look for the word *Kashmir*. I find it just below a photograph of a beautiful pair of green-blue eyes; the rest of the face is covered with a veil.

I know that look.

The young woman is a self-avowed Islamic fundamentalist and looks the part. She swears to the reporter that the status of women in Islam is equal to that of men. She is a leader of Kashmiri Muslim women and has a small female child. The reporter asks her what kind of a life she would like her daughter to have when she grows up.

She says, "I would like her to be the Prime Minister."

I smell a tiger and rose petals.